My Life in
100 Objects

Advance Praise for
My Life in 100 Objects

My Life in 100 Objects is a nonlinear inventory of the self by beat-expressionist-become-revolutionary poet Margaret Randall. Her sense of objecthood is elastic: the expected possessions, yes, writing accoutrements, but also places, photographs, books, art, monuments, artifacts. A medal, a fake passport, a court brief from when the INS tried to deport her. An underused treadmill. She puts it all out there and lets it all in. Even as they stretch all the way back to her childhood in the '40s, or her young adulthood in the '60s, her stories have never been more of the moment: who gets to come to this country, who gets to love whom, and every other hard-won freedom still at stake today.

—**Garrett Caples**, Editor, *City Lights Spotlight*

What a fresh, joyful way to reflect on a life! Try it at home. I sailed through this book with relish, landing on each light and pensive vignette, one after the other, a gathering of image, feeling, and thought. Among many treasures, you are summoned to stone, its enduring beauty in carvings, canyons, ancient structures, beads. Like a cabinet of curiosities, Margaret Randall's beloved objects and places form a record of adventure, inquisitiveness, and inexhaustible love of the world. I am grateful for this book.

—**Mary Louise Pratt**, author of *Imperial Eyes*

Although she is best known as a woman of powerful words and profound political action, Margaret Randall here reveals deep understanding and astute respect for the communicative power and resonance of mute objects. Most of us live with objects that speak to us in personally significant ways.

Most of us don't have the ability to share those silent connections with others. Most of us don't have Margaret's fascinating life that brings such objects to dynamic conversation. Here she invites us to her world of monumental moments of communication with sometimes mundane objects. Reading these brief essays has encouraged me to consider my own personal world as full of chatter, my life told through objects. I am indebted to this great poet for proposing the possibility of finding the poetic links to my psyche and my past. What a gift and a new way of seeing!

—**Andrew Connors**, Director, Albuquerque Museum

Margaret Randall's *My Life in 100 Objects* (and places . . .) is a delightful collection of pictures and long captions narrating the exciting life of one of our progressive heroes. The "objects" range from beloved knickknacks to majestic landscapes to artworks gathered on her extensive travels to artifacts and awards from her career in poetry, photography, and politics. No laundry lists or inconsequential details, just a brilliant octogenarian's loving visual memories.

—**Lucy R. Lippard**, writer, activist, and curator

As I read through this extraordinary gift that Margaret has shared with us, I was sitting at my desk in Spoleto, Italy, and just inches away from my right hand was a small stone given to me by a most sensitive five-year-old boy in my class at the daycare center where I taught in the early '70s. When Olu placed the stone in my hand he said, "It is a mask." That stone and those memories have never left my side. Margaret's *My Life in 100 Objects* will, I believe, touch and resonate with each reader as we move though the objects, images, text and poems that bring us closer to Margaret's life and to our own.

—**Robert Schweitzer**, curator, activist, and teacher

My Life in 100 Objects

Margaret Randall

New Village Press • New York

Published in the United States by New Village Press
bookorders@newvillagepress.net
www.newvillagepress.org
New Village Press is a public-benefit, nonprofit publisher
Distributed by NYU Press

Paperback ISBN: 978-1-61332-114-0
Hardcover ISBN: 978-1-61332-115-7
EBook ISBN: 978-1-61332-116-4
EBook Institutional ISBN: 978-1-61332-117-1

Publication Date: September 2020
First Edition

Library of Congress Cataloging-in-Publication Data

Names: Randall, Margaret, 1936– author.
Title: My life in 100 objects / Margaret Randall.
Other titles: My life in one hundred objects
Description: First edition. | [New York City] : New Village Press, 2020. | Summary: "Author and poet Margaret Randall describes her life through 100 short prose pieces, each written on the image of a different object"—Provided by publisher.
Identifiers: LCCN 2020011249 (print) | LCCN 2020011250 (ebook) | ISBN 9781613321140 (paperback) | ISBN 9781613321157 (hardcover) | ISBN 9781613321164 (ebook) | ISBN 9781613321171 (ebook other)
Subjects: LCSH: Randall, Margaret, 1936– | Women authors, American—20th century—Biography.
Classification: LCC PS3535.A56277 Z46 2020 (print) | LCC PS3535.A56277 (ebook) | DDC 818/.5409 [B]—dc23
LC record available at https://lccn.loc.gov/2020011249
LC ebook record available at https://lccn.loc.gov/2020011250

Cover design: Lynne Elizabeth
Interior design and composition: Leigh McLellan Design

This book is for
Elaine de Kooning,
1918–1989,
mentor and friend.

Contents

INTRODUCTION *What This Book Is and Isn't*   1

OBJECTS

1 Twins, Oldest Known Sculpture, Amman,
   Jordan   11

2 My Father's Metronome   13

3 Portrait of Hannah Pollack   15

4 Old Royal Portable Typewriter, 1940s   17

5 Ammonite Fossil, Madagascar   20

6 Spiral Staircase, Bardo Museum, Tunis,
   Tunisia   22

7 Huipil, Nebaj, Guatemala   24

8 Small Clay Head from Teotihuacán, Mexico   29

9 Days of the Dead Figurine, Mexico   32

10 Rock Art Birth Scene, near Moab, Utah   34

11 First Self-Published Book of Poems,
    Giant of Tears   36

12 Saguaro Cactus, Tucson, Arizona   38

13 Madonna of the Trail, Albuquerque,
    New Mexico   40

14 Appalachian Wooden Apple   42

15 Ceramic Pot from Juan Mata Ortíz, Mexico   44

16 My Father's Claret Cup Cactus   47

17 Ancestral Puebloan Black on White
    Mug (replica)   50

18 Burr Trail, Utah   52

19 Portrait of Margaret by Elaine de Kooning   54

20 Canyon X, Arizona   57

21 Tombs, Petra, Jordan   59

22 Wadi Rum, Jordan   62

23 The Lost Cathedral of Satevó, Copper
    Canyon, Chihuahua, Mexico   64

24 Ceramic Roof Bull, Peru   67

25 Peruvian Weaving Spindle   69

26 Woven Poncho, Cuzco, Peru   71

27 Saffron Strands   73

28 Fake Mexican Passport   75

29 Deportation Hearing Papers   79

30 Nicole Hollander Cartoon   81

31 Ancient Hand Tool, Uruguay   82

32 Hand-Wrought Adz by Aurelio Falero,
    Uruguay   85

33 Piece of Berlin Wall   88

34 Vietnamese Water Puppet   90

35 Red Lacquer Doors, Temple of Literature, Hanoi   92

36 Ho Chi Minh Medal   93

37 Banana Flower, Vietnam   95

38 *The Joy of Cooking*   96

39 My Clay Bread Molds   97

40 Lumi Videla Tapestry, Chile   98

41 Pueblo del Arroyo, Chaco Canyon, New Mexico   102

42 Turquoise Bead, Chaco   105

43 Stone Fountain by Joshua Gannon, Madrid, New Mexico   107

44 Cuban Flag and Santería Tool Necklace   109

45 Martín's Dog Tag, Angola   110

46 Casa de las Américas, Havana, Cuba   112

47 Gregory's Puppet, Cuba   115

48 Girl with Plastic Shoes, Havana   117

49 Grand Canyon, Arizona   120

50 Hermit's Rest, Grand Canyon, Arizona   123

51 Mary Elizabeth Jane Colter Place Setting (replica)   125

52 Pentax K1000 Camera   126

53 Dougga, Tunisia   127

54 Poet of Two Hemispheres Prize, Quito, Ecuador   129

55 Oak Tree House, Mesa Verde, Colorado   133

56 Long House Granary, Mesa Verde, Colorado   136

57 LeConte Glacier Icebergs, Alaska   137

58 Caryatids, Acropolis, Athens, Greece   140

59 Blue-Footed Booby Mother and Chick, Galápagos Islands, Ecuador   143

60 Giant Tortoise, Galápagos Islands, Ecuador   145

61 Marine Iguanas, Galápagos Islands, Ecuador   147

62 Hiking Shoes and Hat   148

63 La Luz Trail, Sandia Mountains, New Mexico   151

64 Plitvice Lakes, Croatia   154

65 Roman Ruin, Butrint, Albania   156

66 EZLN Virgin of Guadalupe, Chiapas, Mexico   159

67 Masks, León, Nicaragua   163

68 Sandinista Certificate, Nicaragua   166

69 Tiny Turquoise Bear Fetish   168

70 "American Girl in Italy" by Ruth Orkin, 1951   170

71 Barbara's Art   173

72 Levi's   175

73 Turquoise Earrings   176

74 Apple Laptop   177

75 *El Corno Emplumado* #26   179

76 Mudhead Kachina Doll, Hopi, Arizona   181

77 Book Bag from City Lights, San Francisco,
California   183

78 Medal for Literary Merit, Chihuahua,
Mexico   185

79 *Time's Language: Selected Poems (1959–2018)*   187

80 *Only the Road / Solo el camino: Eight
Decades of Cuban Poetry*   189

81 *I Never Left Home: Poet, Feminist,
Revolutionary*   191

82 Margaret's and Barbara's Wedding Bands   193

83 Rano Raraku, Rapa Nui   195

84 Tongariki, Rapa Nui   198

85 Rongorongo Board, Rapa Nui (replica)   200

86 Cork Signing Pen   201

87 My Treadmill   202

88 Lioness, Hwange, Zimbabwe   203

89 Honorary Doctorate in Letters, University
of New Mexico   204

90 San Rock Art, KwaZulu-Natal, Drakensberg
Mountains, South Africa   208

91 Maasai Collar, Kenya   210

92 Broken Arch, Ramesseum, Egypt   212

93 Library of Celsus, Ephesus, Turkey   213

94 Uxmal, Mexico   214

95 Great Gallery, Utah   217

96 Kiet Seel, Arizona   219

97 Storyteller Doll, Ada Suina, Cochiti Pueblo,
New Mexico   224

98 Scissors and Ribbon, Beat & Beyond,
New York City   226

99 *When Justice Felt at Home / Cuando la
justicia se sentía en casa*, Vigía Books, Cuba   230

100 Haydée Santamaría Medal, Cuba   233

What This Book Is and Isn't

THE IDEA FOR THIS BOOK must have lodged itself in my consciousness several years ago, when I first read *A History of the World in 100 Objects* by the director of the British Museum, Neil MacGregor.[1] Using only items owned by the museum, that book begins with a two-million-year-old stone chopping tool from the Olduvai Gorge in eastern Africa and ends with a modern-day credit card. In between, 98 other objects come from the farthest reaches of the globe and represent many dozens of cultures, speaking of the visions people had for their lives, the elegant objects they fashioned, and the solutions they innovated to solve problems we still grapple with.

One of the first things that appealed to me about the book was that its author doesn't distinguish between history and so-called pre-history; whether emerging from a time before or after the written word, all featured pieces display the ingenuity, creativity, and beauty of their makers. All are voices that speak to us. The object itself is language. And, in contrast with so many projects carried out by white European men, it isn't Eurocentric in its focus, but embraces items from every corner of the globe. Cultures from cold climates that produced implements from metal or stone

1. Neil MacGregor, *A History of the World in 100 Objects* (New York: Viking Press, 2010).

necessarily had an advantage over those from the tropics or ones made from organic materials, which easily disintegrated with the passage of centuries, even millennia. Still, when unique conditions contributed to the preservation of the latter, the British Museum selection included them. This shouldn't surprise me; the British Empire's colonialist plunder knew no limits.

Although MacGregor's book is one to which I have frequently returned, delighting in what the images say about those who made them, as well as in the descriptive texts, it didn't occur to me to look at my own life in terms of the objects that have shaped it. In 2018 I was putting the finishing touches on my own memoir, *I Never Left Home: Poet, Feminist, Revolutionary*.[2] Writing a memoir involves many decisions regarding life events: what to include, what to leave out, what I wanted to say and how. Objects and places accompanied me in dreams and throughout my waking hours.

It was in this context that I remembered my first typewriter, the 1940's Royal portable, for which I'd earned the money with a paper route at the age of nine. More than seventy years later, I can still smell its faintly oiled matte finish, feel the touch of its keys, their letters and symbols teasing my young fingers from beneath their metal-rimmed clear plastic windows. Thinking about that typewriter naturally led me to contemplate the Apple computer on which I write today. I remembered my first camera, a sturdy Pentax K1000, and the first photograph I made of which I was proud: a small girl with a pile of plastic shoes at the foot of

---

2. Duke University Press, 2020.

a communal staircase in a building at Alamar, the Cuban Revolution's first big housing project. That photograph led me to others that have been important to me, most prominently Ruth Orkin's 1951 "American Girl in Italy," an image that displays everyday misogyny like no other.

I thought of the clay bread molds I've used for more than thirty years and that still fill our home with the aroma of freshly baked loaves. My worn copy of *The Joy of Cooking* and a canvas bag given me the last time I read at iconic City Lights Bookstore in San Francisco. The small 4,000-year-old clay head from Laurette Sejourné's 1960s dig at Teotihuacán. Co-joined clay twin figures at a museum in Amman, Jordan, at 8,500 years considered the oldest surviving sculpture known. A piece of the Berlin Wall. The fake passport I purchased in order to escape Mexico in 1969 and a worn copy of the court transcript from my 1986 deportation hearing. My father's metronome and a claret cup cactus he gave me. The Levi's and turquoise earrings that have become my trademark apparel. The plain gold bands Barbara and I finally bought when we were able to legally marry after living together for twenty-eight years. One object brought to mind another. I carefully photographed them all.

And I quickly realized that places as well as objects have made me who I am: the Serengeti plains where I burst into tears finding our open-sided vehicle surrounded by zebras, giraffes, and other large animals at home in their natural habitat. The ruins of Chaco, Kiet Seel, Petra or Butrint (Albania). The deserts of Tunisia and Jordan. The picture-book delight of Croatia's Plitvice Lakes. Grand Canyon. Rock art sites in Utah or South Africa.

Even the statue of "The Madonna of the Trail" that inhabits one corner of a downtown park in Albuquerque; its artistic style is ugly, its inscription filled with the platitudes of skewed 20th century expansionist discourse. Still, as a young girl growing up in this provincial city, it filled me with admiration for the pioneer women who carried their children with them as they helped open up the west for white settlers (I didn't yet grasp what that westward surge meant for its native inhabitants). These places become objects at the moment my eye meets them head on and my right index finger depresses the camera's shutter; that convergence of time, place, and gaze that renders the moment important in my life.

On the other hand, even if I still possessed them, I probably would not have included such items as my baby book or high school yearbook. Both are cultural products of a homogenized social conformity with which I have identified awkwardly at best: the mother eager to record her child's first step or first word, my school photo among several hundred others, each showing a young person desperately trying to look like every other and filled with the pain of adolescent angst. Here I have preferred to reference objects that spoke to me after I became the woman I am—or that, like the 1940's Royal portable, contributed to making me that woman.

MacGregor's book gathers disparate objects from a vast number of cultures, places, peoples. Mine aims to travel one woman's life to date, through objects, places, and the moments in which these converge. There is no asymmetry here between literate and non-literate history, such as that exemplified by the brutal meeting between

Captain Cook's expedition and the Australian Aboriginals, whose lives were forever changed by that conquest. No inequality between the authoritative captain's log telling of that encounter and a wooden shield dropped by a man in flight after his first experience of gunshot. I have chosen not to arrange my objects chronologically. Yet here I grow from child to young woman, from young woman to older woman and then very old woman. I understand more, but I am always me: singular, shaped by places, things, and moments that converge along a continuous line of living.

My life has been turbulent, sometimes endangered. More than once, actively involved in struggles for social justice, I have had to leave my home in a hurry, taking only the barest necessities. How did some of these objects survive such sudden moves? What caused me to take an ancient Peruvian weaving spindle rather than items that might have served me or my family in a more practical sense? Perhaps only a poet's sensibility.

Size matters. It's been many decades since I sat behind the wheel of my parents' second-hand pale blue 1950's Studebaker. They lent me that car during my teenage years, never knowing I drove it out on the desert, where I'd spend the night as far from civilization as I could get, weaving my own fantasies of pre-Contact romance. The linotype machine and printing press were both important objects in my life. I never owned either, but, if I were to formulate a complete list of items that shaped me, these would have to figure on it.

What determines the importance of an object or place? Their significance necessarily changes over time. They mean one thing when we first come upon them, another as we acquire the retrospective gaze that layers them with connections to different facets of our histories, and yet another when we consider them within a project like this. Our own experience, as well as our acquired understandings of colonialism and the relationship between an object and its environs are all embedded in the things that touch us, changing their meaning. Readers of a book such as this one will also bring their own interpretations to each piece, adding yet another layer. We all arrive with our own antennae, determined by age, gender, class, race, and culture.

When I told him about this project, Suquamish poet friend Cedar Sigo wrote: "I love this idea, it makes clear that certain ceremonial objects also have a collective history. A typewriter is a good example. [...] Interesting to think that the way in which an object is photographed can lend it a loaded or talismanic air, or how does a person breathe an air of history into an object before the camera. Through capturing the dust motes?"

The sense that these objects become talismans is certainly one I recognize. I don't know about the dust motes. Mostly I tried to Photoshop them out of these images, so the object itself would be as unencumbered as possible. But I thought about Cedar's question and realized that, for me, these objects and places come with their histories. Together they have given tangible form to mine. And as they have done so, that task has superimposed itself upon each individual item, imbuing it with a collective power that references identity, time, and place. There is no way I can reproduce in this book the faintly oiled scent of that first typewriter or the way my young fingers felt on its keys, the pride with which I received the Ho Chi Minh medal from my Vietnamese comrades, the excitement surrounding self-publication of my first very bad poetry collection or the satisfaction, almost sixty years later, when my mature *Selected Poems*[3] appeared.

By photographing all these objects and places with as little artifice as possible, I feel that I was allowing them to be fully present, to assume the relevance they have had in my life. I chose a background that most clearly set them off, showed them as they are. In the case of the photographs of places, I chose images I myself have made. This picture takes me back to my first contact with Rapa Nui's moai or the multi-colored sands of Jordan's Wadi Rum. This other evokes my astonished intake of breath on one of the Galápagos Islands as I watched a Blue-Footed Booby teaching her chick to fly.

But there is also the issue of the historic moment. What Rapa Nui's moai meant to me when I visited the island in 2007 was entirely different from what they meant to the people who centuries earlier carved them out of the earth and improbably dragged each giant stone monolith to the shore. We have only the vaguest idea of the culture that produced the creation of those mammoth figures. I photographed them long past their glory: toppling, many half-sunken into the ground or abandoned on their journey to the coast. Yet I have to believe that the figures I saw still held something of their original power.

3. Katherine M. Hedeen and Víctor Rodríguez Núñez, editors, *Time's Language: Selected Poems 1959–2018* (San Antonio: Wings Press, 2018).

Objects and places have always been alive for me. I am as shaped by them as I have been by my parents, lovers, children, friends. Of course, this list of 100 is arbitrary; it might as easily have been 20 or 200. Setting myself a goal of 100 provided a reasonable framework. The book would neither be endless nor too meager. But I feel it is important to say that I might have chosen a different 100. Having moved around as I did, and under the conditions that often surrounded those moves—my underground escape from Mexico in 1969, the US mining of the Nicaraguan port of Corinto in 1984 that prevented me from sending a shipment of my belongings home by sea—has meant that I have lost some precious items along the way: a photograph of my father and me descending Grand Canyon on mules when I was ten, a necklace of beads found in the 1950s at the Peruvian coastal burial crypts of Pachacamác, infant locks of my children's hair. I have searched in vain for some of these things, hoping against hope they would reappear. I have had to make peace with the fact they are now only memories.

Some objects are authentic, others copies or replicas. Two of the items—the 1940's Royal Portable typewriter and the Pentax K1000 camera—aren't actually those I owned but similar models I was able to find online. No longer possessing the originals, there was no way I could photograph them. But they had to be included on my list.

MacGregor's book describes multiple cultures through representative objects. Mine describes one woman's life, thus embracing a very different goal. Still, throughout my years important advances have taken place: from eggbeater to electric mixer, slide rule to calculator, typewriter to computer, film camera to its digital descendant. So, there is also a sense of progression here, a moving line slicing through the history of my particular time.

I also include objects that show that I have often preferred the rudimentary over a much-touted upgrade. For example, I have never been seduced by modern-day bread machines. I have always felt at home kneading and baking bread by hand. I often long to toss my "smart phone" and return to the uncomplicated dependability of an old rotary model. In a similar vein, the photographs of places in this book show that I am more drawn to the sites of ancient cultures than to contemporary buildings or monuments. Over the last few years, I have received some awards that have moved me profoundly. I hope including them doesn't smack of "advertisements for myself." Leaving them out would have been unthinkable.

There is an intimate connection between objects and poems, and perhaps it is easier for a poet to see the poetry in things. This also works in the opposite direction, and so I have occasionally included poems or fragments of poems I hope may help the reader see the object from a range of angles or look beneath it for additional meaning. I hope this book will also succeed in showing you the poetry in objects, how the objects and places that move us breathe their life into ours. I want you to experience those powerful intersections where time, place, and material item—practical or symbolic—come together in such a way as to push or coax life in a new direction, open a window previously closed, expose a newly-felt pulse.

I want to acknowledge the pleasure of working on this book with Lynne Elizabeth of New Village Press. My thanks to everyone at New Village for their enthusiasm and care in helping to make *My Life in 100 Objects* a beautiful object in and of itself.

William Carlos Williams famously said: "No ideas but in things." He was talking about corporality, embodiment, making visible the invisible, tangible the intangible. Here is my personal cartography, a map of my life and time composed of 100 objects, each present in its moment, each speaking out of memory, presence, touch.

1

Twins, Oldest Known Sculpture, Amman, Jordan

THE SHABBY MUSEUM DISPLAYED diverse regional artifacts in dusty glass cases. One drew me immediately, its presence magnetic, compelling. It was a clay sculpture of two figures, co-joined as if they were Siamese twins or perhaps a representation of a single being duplicated to speak of relationship or some other connection. The statue, slightly smaller than life-size, looked to be fashioned from clay: rudimentary, featureless from the neck down,

patched in places. The two sets of eyes were painted, perhaps many times through the centuries, and held very
different expressions. The rest of the figure melted into
a formless shape, limbs and other features disappearing
into an oblong mass. I wondered how this sculpture could
have weathered millennia. A label, in Arabic and English,
claimed it is the oldest known to exist, made 8,500 years
ago.

Questions rose, gentle but insistent. Who made this
evocative sculpture, man or woman, individual or several
people working together? Did it serve a purpose of portrai-
ture, ritual, or one we cannot imagine? What power does
it carry forward through these many years? Was it created
on commission for an individual or for collectivity? Where
was it found and what else was found with it? What has it
been saying, century after century, as time brings it to us?
And how could it have survived so long in such relatively
good condition? The two sets of eyes seem to be daring us
to peel back our own fictitious answers to these questions
and accept the fact that we can never know.

A presence for its own sake.

"Women?" I ask, "men, or maybe neither?"

"Neither," you agree—after a short silence—and I
understand you are not denying them gender, only saying that gender seems irrelevant considering the length
of their journey.[1]

---

1. Section 1 of "Twins," in *Stones Witness (Tucson: University of Arizona
Press*, 2007), 115.

2

My Father's Metronome

MY FATHER PLAYED THE CELLO. He wasn't a great talent but loved the instrument and always struggled to improve. After we moved west, he taught music in the Albuquerque public schools and also had a few private students who came to the house each week; I often heard them reaching to find the right note as Dad patiently guided their fingers.

Growing up, Friday nights at our home were filled with the music of amateur quartets. The click-click-click of Dad's metronome is one of the sounds that defines my childhood. When he died, that pyramid-shaped wooden box was one of the few things of his I wanted, but it was nowhere to be found. Some years later, Barbara bought me this plastic replica, visually similar to the original—even to its simulated wood grain. It lives in my studio, reminding me of my father's gentle steadiness, the dependable rhythm of his love.

3

Portrait of Hannah Pollack

IT MUST HAVE BEEN THE early 1990s when I began having dreams in which I was visited by a female relative, a woman who, from her look and style of dress, had lived at the end of the previous century. She would talk to me about her life, especially its limitations. She made me feel fortunate to be living now. She never told me her name but found her way into a couple of my poems from that era. I included one of them in a reading I gave at Trinity College in Hartford when I still went there as a visiting professor each spring semester.

In Hartford, I'd met some relatives I didn't previously know I had, people on my mother's side of the family with whom my parents had lost touch when they moved us west. It was after this reading that one of them approached and said: "I know who that woman in your dreams is. I even have a photograph of her. And the two of you look very much alike!" That was how I came to understand that my visitor was Hannah Pollack, a great-great-aunt in my maternal lineage. Learning these important details made me feel an even deeper connection.

Hannah rarely enters my dreams these days, but the link through time continues to be powerful. I keep this photograph of her above my writing desk, a constant reminder of the strong women who precede us, each in her own way, making possible our gains in a patriarchal world.

4

Royal Portable Typewriter, 1940s

IT TOOK ME LONGER THAN my contemporaries to master reading and writing, but from the time I learned, I knew I wanted to be a writer. And, as a typical product of middle-class America, I believed writers had typewriters. I was nine years old when I started asking my parents for one. Their two requirements were that I work to earn half the cost of the machine, which was $150, and that I learn to touch-type.

The first requirement presented problems. As a preteen, I had few money-making skills. With insistence and a few lies, however, I wrangled a neighborhood newspaper route, getting up before dawn each morning to collect my allotted pile of papers, roll them neatly, and secure each with a length of sewing thread. Then I arranged them in bags that straddled the back of my red Mohawk bike. As the summer wore on, my aim improved, and I easily managed to hit the stoop at almost every house. A girl with a paper route wasn't favorably looked upon in our stuffy upper-class Scarsdale neighborhood. Not in the 1940s. But I persisted. I also babysat for those who could be induced to trust "a mature nine-year-old." And I remember selling cookies door-to-door.

I can still evoke the day I'd finally managed to save $75. My mother and father proudly took me to the store where I'd seen the machine of my dreams and it became mine. Then they helped me send away for a typing course, predecessor to today's online self-learning kits. I remember it came with a little card that simulated the arrangement of the keys. You propped it up and were instructed to look at it rather than at the keyboard as you practiced J-U-G jug, J-U-G jug, followed by other combinations of letters designed to accustom your fingers to the positions of each. It was important to develop a steady rhythm by practicing to a ditty called "The Syncopated Clock" which I played over and over on our family phonograph. The idea was to close your eyes, or at least not peek at the keys. Slow and steady, the accompanying booklet said. It wasn't long before I passed my first proficiency test with a score of 60 words per minute.

Learning to touch-type at such an early age has served me well, although not in the way our high school typing classes intended. My dream was to be a writer, not a secretary. After the Royal portable, I had an ancient Remington

Rand, and later a sleekly designed Olympia. It wasn't until I was in my late forties and had returned to live in the US that I graduated to a computer. And many years later, I switched from a PC to an Apple.

I still easily conjure the faintly oiled scent, matte finish, and clear little plastic windows covering each key. Inserting a clean sheet of paper onto the roller, straightening it and then bringing its top edge even beneath the metal guard that fell into place to hold it down. The warning sound of the little bell as I'd get to the end of a line and take the accustomed swing at the handle that moved me to the beginning of the next. These automatic motions provided a kind of aimless interlude between pages, in which you could ponder what you'd write next. I will never forget the texture of onion skin second sheets, the red and black ribbon as it gradually grew dimmer after producing many pages, the messy white-out that came in a small bottle with a tiny brush.

A pre-digital era. We, not our phones, were expected to be smart.

I learned to type almost as fast as I could think.

5

Ammonite Fossil, Madagascar

BARBARA AND I HAVE BEEN friends for many years
with poet V.B. Price and his artist wife Rini Price.[1] We get
together over a meal a couple of times a month, sharing
new work, critiquing one another, and appreciating having people with whom there is the sort of trust that allows
for reading and talking about very incipient texts. We enjoy being part of a collective process that moves from idea
to published piece.

V.B. is a collector: of art, indigenous artifacts, rocks,
shells, fossils. We have been the lucky recipients of several
of these. This large snail-like fossil is one. It is a halved

---

1. Rini Price, 1941–2020.

ammonite that lived from between 240 and 265 million years ago, at the time of the dinosaurs. It measures six inches wide by five and three-quarters inches high. I have to imagine how it may have moved through murky waters in an era so remote as to be almost unimaginable.

V.B. tells me he believes this particular ammonite was cleaned up and polished in Madagascar. He says its age, coupled with the survival of its form, makes it a talisman of time for him. How time works changes everything, ourselves included. He also feels this fossil is evidence that the cosmos has as one of its properties the sensation of beauty, the actuality of being smitten by someone or thing, the reality of compassion and other manifestations of the limbic system. This gives the cosmos a numinous quality that exists beyond doctrine or dogma or "book."

I know this ancient ammonite must have moved gracefully then and is beautiful in its petrified stat—a reminder that we do not need to understand everything about an object to feel drawn to its power.

The spiral is a female form.

6

Spiral Staircase, Bardo Museum, Tunis, Tunisia

THE AMMONITE'S SPIRAL FORM is echoed in this contemporary stairwell at the Bardo Museum in Tunis. The Bardo houses a magnificent collection of mosaics, representing all eras and styles in a country known for its riches in that artform. No artificial lighting illuminates the Bardo's exhibitions; the natural brilliance from sky-lights and windows bathes all in perfect luminescence, making you feel you are strolling through ruins where in-tricate mosaics can still be seen in their natural setting on ancient walls and floors. We spent hours at the Bardo and felt we could have spent many more. We were as dazzled by the intelligence of its architecture as by the wealth of its collection. This photograph, taken from a high floor looking down to lower ones, became as much of an object to me as any of the masterworks in the museum's collection.

7

Huipil, Nebaj, Guatemala

SINCE GOING TO LIVE IN Latin America in 1961, I was drawn to huipiles, the richly embroidered blouses worn by indigenous women in Mexico and Guatemala. I wore them over Levi's, taking comfort in their loose-fitting ease and inspiration from their fine needlework that tells a story.

In the early 2000s, traveling through Central America, I wanted to go to the Guatemalan mountain village of Nebaj, home of a particularly beautiful huipil. Each version's design is unique to the area in which it is worn. These items of clothing are not simply works of art; they tell us something about the women who wear them: where they are from; whether they are married, widowed, or single; how many children they have. Maps upon which the stories of a life are woven in colored threads.

I once asked a native woman if she was troubled by outsiders such as myself wearing huipiles. "No," she said, "but we don't want you wearing our skirts." Those skirts are wraparound lengths of homespun cloth tucked under at the waist or secured by a woven belt. I was stunned; the huipil seemed so much more of a personal statement than the skirt.

Our young Guatemalan guide had never been to Nebaj, but cheerfully set out with us on the nine-hour journey. When we got to the village, he would help us look for the huipiles. But when we arrived, we found the people to be remote, turning away in silence even when our guide asked where we might find what we were looking for. He was Guatemalan, but apparently almost as much of an outsider as we were. Clearly, this village didn't trust outsiders, probably with good reason. We'd been through the central market and had stopped a dozen or so locals in our search, when we began to think we might have made this trip in vain. We had almost decided to leave.

Then my partner, Barbara, spotted a couple of children playing in a park. Her schoolteacher experience came to the fore and she engaged with them. After a while, she repeated the question we'd been asking of everyone we saw: "Do you know where we might be able to find the beautiful huipiles made here?" The children took us to their mother, who was welcoming. She invited us to her home for lunch. Her own mother, an ancient-looking woman whose face was a map of creviced skin, said she was too old to party now. She might be willing to sell us her special party huipil.

Walking through Nebaj's narrow streets accompanied by locals made us feel more relaxed. We arrived at the family home, one dark room in a warren of such rooms and connecting courtyards overrun by small domesticated animals—chickens and guinea pigs—and a number of naked toddlers. One child squatted every few minutes to deposit a puddle of diarrhea on the mud floor. Our host ushered us into her personal space—a single all-purpose room—and immediately put a pot of water to boil on a wood stove. She took several enamel bowls from a cupboard and began wiping them with a frayed towel. She could offer us some noodles, she said. The water they were cooked in was flavored with a bit of tomato.

Put off by the unsanitary conditions, Barbara and I exchanged a worried glance. Our host caught sight of our hesitation and assured us we didn't need to eat. She understood. Mortified, we told her no, we were looking forward to what she was preparing. We finished the bowls of ramen-like noodles which were actually quite tasty. Silently, we promised ourselves we would never again reject such hospitality, even if it made us ill. It didn't make us ill, only ashamed of our own classism.

After our shared meal, the older woman opened the bottom drawer of a large armoire and took out a neatly folded huipil. Even after years of use, its beauty was radiant. We asked how much and didn't try to bargain with this woman who was offering us her most treasured piece of clothing. This is how I acquired this exquisite Nebaj huipil, made for special occasions in the life of a woman who no longer felt she could look forward to celebrating them.

MIRRORS

This woman, toothless at thirty-eight,
laughs at her sister's parchment gaze,
knows the angry row of curls
nudging her baby's ear
but is oblivious to the camera's claim to her.
She cannot find her face
on the surface of this photograph.
There are no mirrors in her hills.
Mirrors chased through your childhood
making you watchful and sad.
By tenth grade they gave back Sears Charm School,
father's unwelcome eyes.
Threat of fingers. The belt.
That thick secret.
Now you avoid them, pronounce relief
at the thought of a world where mirrors aren't.
My own mirror taunts a canyon of mist
where Vogue silhouettes hum off-key melodies.
Food uneaten on the plate.
Melted. Changed. The real body
reflecting that other willowed stance.
Perfect skin. And especially the graceful neck.
How I've longed for the grace of that neck.

That woman who does not recognize
her image in the photograph—
can we say she has never seen herself?
Where is the mirror
unbruised enough to tell us who we are?[1]

1. *Dancing with the Doe* (Albuquerque: West End Press, 1992), 32.

8

Small Clay Head from Teotihuacán, Mexico

WHEN MY SMALL SON Gregory and I arrived in Mexico in the fall of 1961, the French-Mexican anthropologist Laurette Sejourné was one of the first people we met. We quickly became close friends. At the time, Laurette was supervising an archeological dig at the Palace of Butter-flies, one of the residential areas adjacent to the pyramids at Teotihuacán, about an hour northeast of the city by car. She had a team of workmen engaged in retrieving ordinary household as well as ceremonial objects. Each Wednesday she would drive out to assess what they'd unearthed since she'd been there last.

Soon she invited us to come along. She would pack a picnic lunch, pick us up in her gray Peugeot, and we would leave the busy metropolis and drive into the countryside, which in those years was a great deal less settled than it is today. When we arrived at the site, we'd make ourselves comfortable in that place that exuded the still-living spirit of another time. And we would observe Laurette as she decided which pieces to bring back to the city for cataloging and further study, which to leave on site. I had no idea then of my friend's brilliance in her field, of the ways in which she stretched or even rejected the archeological assumptions of those years. One day she gave me this small clay head, perhaps from a child's doll. It measures two inches by an inch and a half. She said it was a minor artifact that would be disposed of or returned to the earth if no one wanted it.

It is not minor to me, but symbolic of a people and their culture. I have kept it close ever since.

LAURETTE AT TEOTIHUACÁN

You walk with small steps, back absolutely erect,
a picnic basket swinging on your arm.
From the painted cane of that basket
dark breads and rich pâtés emerge
along with monogrammed linen,
butter knives and a thermos of good tea.
Your weekly visit to meet with local diggers

who work according to your instruction
and design, the way you contemplate
four thousand years in a perfect brown clay pot,
decide it will travel home with you
or remain among these onsite findings.
You try to explain this Palace of Butterflies,
how ordinary houses spill their secrets,
completing a city
crowned by pyramids. Sun. Moon.
A world you see but struggle to explain
against official rhetoric.
My small son plays along the trenches,
laughs in fresh earth, runs back to us
lured by the scent of roasted chicken
or stuffed chayote when it's time for lunch.
Beneath his blonde curls
old eyes absorb each glint and shadow.
Teotihuacán, where you offer imagination
and I begin to learn what it means
to understand too much
in a world that values tradition
and the ideas of men
over female wisdom, female risk.[1]

---

1. *Ruins* (Albuquerque: University of New Mexico Press, 2011), 76.

9

Days of the Dead Figurine, Mexico

EACH YEAR, ON OCTOBER 31ST, November 1st and 2nd, Mexicans celebrate death. Many families construct small altars in their homes. Days of the Dead festivities date back to Aztec times, when they honored the goddess Mictecacihuatl. Today, families set high tables or shelves—even the top of a standing cabinet or TV will do—on which photographs of those who have died during the previous year are prominently displayed. The altars are piled high with the departed one's favorite foods, little sugar skulls, special breads, and other seasonal dishes and drinks. Paper flowers adorn the arrangement. There is an air of mourning but also of festivity.

Along the floor, running from the street through the front door to the base of the altar, a line of *cempasúchil*, or marigolds, marks the way so that the souls of the dead will know where to go. Days of the Dead observances are held in a number of other Latin American countries, in Mexican neighborhoods in the United States, and as far away as Australia. In some regions of Mexico, the celebrations are unique, as at the tiny island of Janitzio on Lake Patzcuaro in the state of Michoacán, where locals wind their way to a cemetery at the island's highest point carrying huge brightly painted *ofrendas* made of hardened bread dough.

In recent times, Days of the Dead altars have also taken on sociopolitical issues such as domestic violence or the immense numbers of citizens murdered by the drug cartels. This is in sharp contrast with our Halloween when children dressed as witches and ghosts go from house to house asking for handouts of candy. Rather than trafficking in fear, ridiculing death, or turning it into a bizarre parody, Mexicans confront it head-on, opening a space in which to feel and talk about the phenomenon.

I was given this small figurine at one of the many Days of the Dead celebrations I've attended. The iconic death character is offering pieces of fruit from a platter bearing a colorful selection. It is one of several examples of popular art that remind me of less fearful or rigid ways of contemplating the inevitable.

10

Rock Art Birth Scene, near Moab, Utah

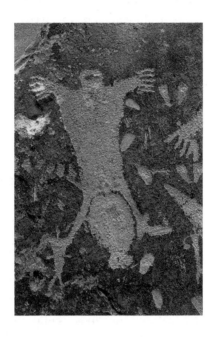

FOR YEARS, BARBARA AND I searched for rock art throughout the US American Southwest. Utah has many sites. There's even a guidebook listing all those on public lands, with precise instructions on how to get to each.[1] Every hike was worth the effort. Most sites display some combination of humans and animals: hunting scenes or

---

1. Dennis Slifer, *Guide to Rock Art of the Utah Region* (Santa Fe: Ancient City Press, 2000).

more peaceful portrayals. Sometimes you can spot these panels of petroglyphs or pictographs as you approach. Sometimes they are half-hidden, surprising you as you turn a corner or peer into a crevice of rock. We often wondered if we should call these manifestations art. Were they etched into or painted on stone as adornment, message, signpost, record, or with a purpose we cannot imagine today? Who created them, and for whom?

On a boulder just outside Moab, Utah, this rendition of a woman giving birth is brutal in its figurative realism, clear in what it depicts. The mother's arms as well as her legs are spread wide. Her baby has descended the birth canal and is already halfway out in the world. Surrounding the figure, prominent drops — blood? tears? — enhance the scene.

I have never seen another rock art image of a woman giving birth. In the middle of that lonely field, the power of the image sprang from its red rock surface to my astonished eyes, linking to my own memories of childbirth.

11

First Poetry Collection, Giant of Tears

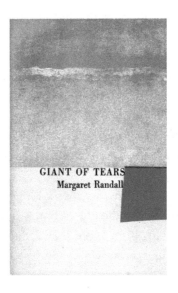

EVEN THE TITLE IS EMBARRASSING. I was twenty-two years old, having recently arrived in the big city, working hard and willing myself to be a poet. A few of my poems were accepted by the little magazines of the day. Soon I was invited to read at one of the Greenwich Village coffee houses. Several of my painter friends offered to illustrate my first self-published collection with their already accomplished drawings. I've always wondered what they saw in the very incipient artist I was then, and I continue to marvel at their generosity. This little book defines me whether I want it to or not. It exists in the world, marking the beginning of my poetic journey. It stands among my list of objects almost as penance.

I vaguely remember paying a printer out in Brooklyn $500 to help me produce a modest number of copies. Maybe three hundred or so? I no longer remember. With my meager secretarial and artist's model income, it must have taken me a while to save that sum. Other memories surrounding the little book are clearer: the spider monkey that printer kept in a large cage to the left of his press, the clunky Varitype machine he taught me to operate. And later, walking the streets with copies of the finished product which I hoped to leave at local bookstores. Some stores took a few on consignment, others paid upfront, conscious of how important a few dollars could be to a young writer new in the city.

I cringe when I try to read those early poems. Then I remind myself that owning one's trajectory is part of revealing oneself honestly, a necessary exercise if one believes, as I do, that we don't immediately inhabit our full creative selves but move into them slowly, through hard work, discipline, and a gradual ability to claim our voice. This is an object that has defined me more for what it symbolizes in terms of pointing to the need for improvement than in terms of achievement or pride. Still, it is an important stop on my personal journey.

12

Saguaro Cactus, Tucson, Arizona

SAGUARO CACTUSES ARE LIKE giant beings, dotting southern Arizona's high desert landscape. They endow Tucson's environs with a particular aura. They can live up to 200 years and achieve heights of 40 feet. Often, they branch out, growing as many as 20 or 25 arms, although some never do grow arms and simply rise off the desert floor like sentinels; these are called spears. When they die, saguaros disintegrate into hollowed-out lattices of spiny wood. In the spring, they may acquire one or more large blooms. Small birds sometimes nest in their flesh.

I have walked among the saguaros often, communing with them in different seasons. If you get far enough from the highway or some other familiar landmark, you can easily become lost in the mesmerizing desert heat. The giants raise their arms as if to beckon or embrace but lead you only to yourself. Although I don't own a saguaro nor, as is true about humans, do I believe they can be owned, their existence has helped define my life.

13

Madonna of the Trail, Albuquerque, New Mexico

WHEN I WAS GROWING UP in Albuquerque in the 1940s and '50s, this monument stood in a different city park. I never did learn why it was moved. I remember walking past as a preteen, immune to its clichéd presentation and unaware that phrases such as "the primitive west" were colonialist at best: the unexamined discourse of an era in which I would not have known how to question such ignorant definitions. On the contrary, this *Madonna of the Trail*—one of several such monuments erected in western cities—elicited a thrill of identification in me. As a young woman, I already sensed the restrictions placed on my gender. Any gesture that seemed to revere those women who preceded me, and who I knew had faced painful obstacles simply in order to survive, inspired an intimate pride.

I remember calling this stone image "The Pioneer Woman." I wasn't privy to a religious upbringing, and the word "Madonna" wasn't part of my vocabulary. No, this was The Pioneer Woman, my Pioneer Woman, and for a very long time she remained strong in my consciousness. An ugly monument giving me something I needed.

> [...] I used to want to stand and look at that woman
> for hours.
> I never did.
> My parents dispensed with it as bad sculpture.
> In our history books the pioneer mother
> pioneer woman was flat page after flat page
> she came to America to the new land
> in a sailing vessel salt pork and careening decks
> riding the waves.
> If she lived, she was already a heroine.
> The rest was a collection of phrases repeated
> and we repeated them dutifully:
> she-worked-the-land-with-her-man-
> reared-her-children-fought-off-savage-Indians-
> was-god-fearing-man-fearing-and-good,
> and those who weren't
> were not in the books [...][1]

---

1. "Motherhood." In *Carlota: Prose and Poems from Havana* (Vancouver: New Star Books, 1978), 42.

14

Appalachian Wooden Apple

IN 1957 I MET THE PAINTER Elaine de Kooning, who had come to Albuquerque as a visiting professor in the University of New Mexico's art department. We became instant friends. I identified with her free spirit, some-one who put creativity at the center of her life. And she was the first woman I knew who seemed able to ignore the gender strictures of the era, although I couldn't yet know at what personal cost. When she returned to New York, I followed.

Elaine always bought art from younger or lesser-known artists. She understood they needed the money, but that the acknowledgment and encouragement were just as important. She'd even developed a formula for herself:

each time she sold a painting, she would spend roughly a quarter of what she made on such a purchase. Something else I learned from Elaine was to reject the supposed difference between fine art and craft. A piece of art was good or bad; the only distinction that mattered.

When Elaine traveled, which was often, she always came home with gifts for her friends. If she saw a particularly beautiful or interesting handmade object, she would buy a dozen or more and spread them around. This is a life-size wooden apple she brought back from Appalachia. She said she found an elderly woman carving them by the side of a country road. At first glance, the cut and teeth marks seem real enough to invite a taste. The inner brown appears to be the fruit's flesh exposed to the air.

I've kept this wooden apple because I love it, loved Elaine, and because it reminds me to laugh at the false dichotomy between fine art and craft.

15

Ceramic Pot from Juan Mata Ortíz, Chihuahua, Mexico

NOT FAR FROM THE TOWN of Casas Grandes and the ruins of Paquimé on Chihuahua's vast northern plain lies the small village of Juan Mata Ortíz. When we visited in the 1990s it still had no hotel or restaurant, just a few dusty streets where potters would call the occasional visitors into their homes to show off their wares. Some of the homes were surprisingly well-constructed and spacious considering the state of the village overall.

In the 1960s, a villager named Juan Quezada labored on the railroad. On his long walk to and from work, he kicked the earth beneath his boots and unearthed pieces of pottery produced many hundreds of years earlier by his indigenous ancestors. The discovery made him wonder about the rich clays available on that desert, how his forebears had fired them, and the designs they had used. Quezada began to experiment until he found his own clay deposits, evolved successful firing methods, and created unique designs. He was meticulous and immensely talented. In time, he became a world-renowned potter, putting his tiny village on the map.

By the time we discovered Juan Mata Ortíz, a dozen younger potters had learned from the master. Quezada, who sold examples of his art for $5,000 in Tokyo and New York, wanted progress for his village. He taught, invested, opened a small gallery, and encouraged a neighbor to establish a place where visitors could get something to eat. A couple of local families conditioned spare rooms to receive guests. Before these innovations, tourists had no choice but to stay in the much larger nearby town of Casas Grandes.

We would drive down from Albuquerque with empty cardboard boxes and plenty of newsprint we could use to cushion the bowls we knew we would purchase for $5, $10 or $20 each. We enjoyed spending a day going into people's homes, sharing a cup of coffee, observing their crude firing processes. Whether or not we bought, they were invariably welcoming.

Their ovens were nothing more than a cow-dung fire covered by a zinc washtub. They were able to complete a low-level firing while we watched. Juan Quezada's sister, Consolación, made the largest pots in the village; that was her claim to fame. The one I've included in my 100 objects is by a young man named Fernando, who specialized in the traditional white on black. Other local potters were more adventurous with their motifs, sometimes incorporating patterns of stylized fish and a palette of earth colors. They all knew that value lay in the thinness of clay walls and perfection of form. They painted with the finest of brushes and sanded the surface of their pots with small stones in the manner of their ancestors.

Today, Juan Mata Ortíz is on every Mexican tourist map. Its best potters earn a good living from their work, which is exported to galleries throughout the world. The village itself has benefitted from Quezada's loyalty. And I remember a time before everything changed.

16

My Father's Claret Cup Cactus

MY FATHER PAID CLOSE attention to society's do's and don'ts. He stayed within the lines. On the rare occasions when he dared to cross them, it was because he could no longer embrace docility. A deep passion would suddenly break through his quiet demeanor, and you always delighted in the moment. Such was the case after he visited us in Cuba in the 1970s. A public school music teacher in an impoverished system, he was excited by that small island country's efforts to provide a music education to all the children who wanted one. He was moved by students who had to replace their violin or cello strings with electrical wire but practiced enthusiastically. In Albuquerque he took up collections among his friends to buy them proper strings, sheet music, even the occasional instrument. I knew that he would understand it best if I let him discover the Revolution through a music teacher's sensibility.

I saw this passion in my father again when he marched against New Mexico's right to work law and, not long before his death, when he stood beside me on our city's civic plaza one bitterly cold January night to protest the 1991 invasion of Iraq. I can still feel the warmth of his arthritic fingers grasping mine, the comfort of his principled accompaniment.

For years, Dad walked his dog every morning in the foothills to the east of the city. Little signs at the trail head near his house warned against digging up native plants on National Forest land. My father would have been the first to obey such signs. But he couldn't resist this tiny claret cup cactus. I had recently returned from a quarter century in Latin America. My parents had given me a piece of land next door to theirs and were helping me build a house. One day Dad showed up with the little cactus, its roots wrapped in damp newsprint. We carefully transplanted it to what would always remain the wild untended landscape others might have coaxed into a proper garden.

That cactus took root and bloomed each year. When my parents were forced to move into town, where they could get the daily care they needed, Barbara and I also chose to leave what had become a wealthy conservative neighborhood for one among whose inhabitants we felt more comfortable. We took the claret cup with us, hoping it would be able to survive yet another relocation.

Now it continues to thrive in our small city back yard. My father has been gone for more than two decades. Whenever a thirsty bee visits the cactus's seasonal bloom, I like to imagine his spirit has come to see how we're all getting on.[1]

---

1. We have moved yet again, this time without the claret cup. I carry it now only in memory.

17

Ancestral Puebloan Black on White Mug (replica)

I BOUGHT THIS REPLICA of an Ancestral Puebloan mug many years ago at the gift shop at Mesa Verde. There it stood, surrounded by refrigerator magnets, key chains, t-shirts, and cheap silver and turquoise jewelry—some of it local, some mass-produced in Taiwan. The carefully made reproduction was dignified in its simulation of an original piece of Mesa Verde black-on-white created between 1150 and 1280 AD, its shape, heft, and polished surface all reminiscent of its ancient forebear. It didn't pretend to be authentic, but to someone like myself, who will never own or even hold the real thing, it spoke in a voice I heard. I gave it to Barbara, and she has had it in her studio ever since.

The mug's neck displays the iconic cloud motif alternating with a field of small squares that resemble a modern-day crossword puzzle, except that small black dots rather than letters fill the white squares. The base of the bowl is covered with a triangular pattern of lines. But the most interesting part of the mug is its handle, fashioned in the form of an elongated and stylized mountain sheep. The entire receptacle is a graceful representation of the culmination of whiteware ceramic technology and decorative conventions typical of pottery produced at the height of Ancestral Puebloan life on the Colorado Plateau.

Seeing a reproduction or replica in our home, friends have sometimes remarked: "Oh, it's a copy." Since I have rarely dreamed of owning an original artifact of worth — don't believe they should reside outside museums or even outside the sites where they originated — I have always appreciated a carefully made reproduction. It is a way for a lover of the culture to touch, hold, caress something as close as possible to the original.

18

Burr Trail, Utah

THIS IS THE FIRST ENTRY in this book where place becomes object, the photograph of a landscape or building evoking an instant I hold as if it were a material thing. Not static, but capturing that moment in which gaze, season, time of day, and click of the camera's shutter come together in a way that speaks to me of who I am. Not an object in the conventional sense, this instant exemplifies my love for the dramatic red rock canyon landscape of the American Southwest.

As you leave the Lake Powell area and head toward Capitol Reef, you find yourself in this wild wonderland.

Immense multicolor cliffs rise beside the narrow unpaved road. There is almost no other traffic, yet you hesitate to stop for a picture. If you did, it's unlikely you'd be able to capture the full feeling of this rugged land. It is more than the eye can see, more than human consciousness can absorb.

19

Portrait of Margaret
by Elaine de Kooning

AFTER FOLLOWING ELAINE to New York City in the late 1950s, I would often stop by her Broadway loft. She painted and we talked. Sometimes she was in the middle of sketching a friend, one of the many works that would eventually comprise her large collection of signature portraits. She moved quickly, had the ability to capture in a few sure strokes the expression or body gesture that defined her model. Artists, critics, sports, and entertainment figures showed up on her canvasses. Her official likeness of John F. Kennedy was the first of a sitting president to be commissioned to a woman artist.

One afternoon I dropped in at her studio and Elaine asked me to pose. In rapid succession she did seven small paintings on paper, all in tones of grays and blacks. I remember the moment well. I was pregnant with my son, Gregory and was wearing a tent-like shift I had stitched myself. I still smoked back then, and in one of the portraits hold a cigarette. Another is an almost abstract rendering of hair piled on top of my head, eyebrows, and one long earring. This one she may have done from memory. The resemblance is unmistakable.

I used one from this series as a frontispiece in *Ecstasy is a Number*, my second book of poems.[1] Elaine let me choose one of the originals, gave another to my parents, and one eventually ended up in the permanent collection of the National Museum of Women in the Arts in Washington, DC. Years later, when I was involved in the struggle to regain my US citizenship, she had yet another made into a high-quality poster. She donated the image and we sold the posters to raise money for my defense.

It was when she was preparing to have that image reproduced as a poster that the issue arose around when she had painted it. Elaine often signed and dated her work only when it sold, or when she took it out years after having made it to send to a show. I stood there watching as she scrawled her characteristic EdeK at the bottom of that image, and then added a date: '63. I knew I hadn't sat for

---

1. *Ecstasy is a Number* (New York: self-published, 1961).

that portrait in 1963. I left New York for Mexico in the fall of 1961. I also remembered having been pregnant with Gregory, who was born in October 1960. No, 1960 was the year she painted that series, not 1963. I argued my case, but Elaine was adamant. When she was convinced of something, it was impossible to change her mind.

That poster went out into the world bearing a date that was off by three years, just as each of the other paintings in that series also bear the wrong date. Elaine died in 1989, and in 2015 the Smithsonian's National Portrait Gallery hosted a major exhibition of her portraits. One of that series she'd painted of me was included in the show. I had an opportunity to discuss the date with the curator and was pleased when she acknowledged my memory of it both on the wall label and in the catalog.

My parents are gone. The friend who owned the abstract image generously gifted it to me a few years back. So I now own three of the seven original portraits. One, as I say, is at the National Museum of Women's Art. I often wonder where the other three are.

This small painting speaks to me of a particularly intense and beautiful time in my life.

20

Canyon X, Arizona

STANDING WITHIN THE EARTH is very different from standing on it. Vast caverns with their stalagmites and stalactites, ice caves, dark recesses, or slot canyons that embrace you in their undulating folds. You become so much a part of where you are that claustrophobia is unlikely. In northern Arizona, two stretches of Antelope Canyon allow you to drop down into underground slots where light seeping through brief openings on the surface casts shadows that accentuate rock forms powerful in their ever-changing mystery. Navajo children stand sentinel at the entrance and help you drop the few feet into the underground world, charging a few dollars for the experience.

Canyon X, on private rather than Indian land, is more of a commercial venture. You must make a reservation online, meet up with your guide in Page, Arizona, and travel with him to the site. The advantage is having the underground canyon to yourself, with time to explore conditions and angles. Each moment of changing light reveals a new image. The experience of being physically embraced by the earth leaves a lasting impression.

21

Tombs, Petra, Jordan

IN 2004 I TOOK ONE OF MY grandsons to the Museum of Natural History in New York. The featured exhibit was about Petra, the mysterious Nabataean ruin in Jordan that was first settled in 312 BC. I was hooked. Upon my return to Albuquerque, I told Barbara we must see Petra for ourselves.

I began researching trips online, but soon found that no US travel service took people to Jordan back then. A couple of brief excursions were tacked onto religious pilgrimages to the Holy Land, but that wasn't what I wanted. I hoped to spend several days exploring Petra, and also visit other parts of what seemed to be a fascinating country. I wasn't interested in the spot where Jesus supposedly was baptized, or others of biblical fame. When I found a small travel agency in the village of Petra itself, I wrote and inquired about the possibility that it might help me design such a trip. Soon I was corresponding with someone—I couldn't tell by the name whether man or woman—who seemed willing to help us visit the places that interested us.

A vehicle with guide and driver. A few days in Amman. Visits to some of the magnificent castles on the desert, and downtime on the desert itself. The Dead Sea and environs. And a couple of women's crafts cooperatives; I'd read about Queen Noor and the changes she'd made for Jordan's women. But mostly Petra: not a quick in-and-out, but several days to explore the ruin and its outlier sites.

I finally asked and was told my correspondent was a man. When we'd come to an agreement for what seemed like the perfect two weeks, I asked him if he could give me a secure site; I was ready to commit and wanted to give him my credit card number. "No," he replied, "we wouldn't think of charging you before you complete the trip. How could we know if you'd been satisfied? Just bring the money in cash and you can pay us on your last day." It was $3,000 for the two of us, travel, translation, entrance fees to historic sites, hotels and almost all meals included. And they did indeed refuse to take our money until the last day of our trip.

Our guide was Madi, a Bedouin who had been born and grew up in the caves around Petra. He knew the area and spoke good English. He met our flight in Amman and, for the next two weeks, accompanied us around his country. He was knowledgeable and forthcoming, innately misogynist, but possessed a somewhat mitigating kindness and sense of humor, as well as a unique take on history.

One day we passed a rock formation by the side of the road and he pointed it out to us as "Lot's wife, after she was turned into a pillar of salt!"

We explored desert castles where we were the only people within miles, hiked and slept on the desert, savored local delicacies, and waited for Madi on a village rooftop for more than an hour one day while he tracked down, butchered, and prepared a delicious chicken for our lunch. But the climax of the trip was Petra. You enter through the narrow Siq or quarter-mile canyon, at the end of which a first view of the ruin comes into view. It is a magical experience. Human and animal figures emerge from the walls in various states of damage caused by time and weather. A narrow water canal running the length of this entrance passage reveals the complex engineering that sustained Petra at the height of its glory.

Words fall short in describing Petra's massive scale, peaceful aura, more than 800 great buildings carved from pink rock, or the multicolor interiors of the caves where people like Madi once lived. Not that long before, the Jordanian government had moved these human settlements to modern housing a few miles distant. Despite having access to electricity, running water, and other amenities, people still resisted the change.

Our first day at Petra, Madi invited us into a cave where one of his uncles had a tea room. We sat for a while, sipping small glasses of the sweet drink. Our last day at the ruins we returned to that tea room on our own. We expected to buy our tea this time around and were surprised when our host refused to take our money. "Hospitality," he said, "is part of the Petra experience."

22

Wadi Rum, Jordan

ON NEW YEAR'S EVE, Petra Moon—the local travel agency through which we'd arranged our trip to Jordan—invited all its guests who were in the country at the time to spend a night on the desert. This particular desert is called Wadi Rum. Twenty or so small Coleman tents were arranged in a semicircle. Each had room for two people on narrow cots. Facilities were rudimentary. Our hosts played lutes, danced, and cooked lamb and vegetables in a pit fire covered by desert sand. As the sun set, all the desert's colors bloomed in rapidly changing majesty.

The next day, Madi asked us if we wanted to hike. We said yes. He pointed us in one direction and said he would be waiting for us about a mile away with a picnic lunch. We set off, soon finding ourselves surrounded by landscape that gave no clue as to destination. We gave ourselves to the beauty of the land, confident our guide wouldn't abandon us. An hour or so later we spotted his tiny figure, frantically waving his arms in an indication of where we should head. After a delicious meal, we were surprised to see him toss the leftovers onto the sand. "They will be gone within minutes," he explained. "Everything organic is devoured by the animals living here."

23

The Lost Cathedral of Satevó, Copper Canyon, Chihuahua, Mexico

AT THE BOTTOM OF Copper Canyon, about five kilometers from the village of Batopilas in the even smaller community known as Satevó, stands a brick and plaster church known as The Lost Cathedral. We walked through brilliant countryside. Groups of children pushed hoops that looked to be old bike-wheel frames. When they reach adulthood, some of these children may become the famous runners who skim the earth barefoot, sometimes one hundred miles at a stretch. Tarahumaras have won foot races as far away as Colorado.

A graceful bridge spans the river, and suddenly there it is: the lost cathedral, sometimes called Iglesia San Miguel de Satevó. A four-tiered bell tower is topped by a graceful filigree cross. The lines of the rest of the structure are simple but elegant.

Records have disappeared, and sources vary wildly on the origin, age, and just about everything else about this church. Some say it was built as early as the 16th century, others after 1740. Some claim the Franciscans were responsible for its construction, but most believe it was the Jesuits—who are also rumored to have built a handful of other churches hidden throughout this rugged land. The very existence of the lost cathedral becomes a mystery when it is pointed out that Satevó was never much larger than it is today, a few modest houses scattered in an improbable location. Why such a large edifice? Who said mass here throughout the centuries? Who came to pray?

Locals tell us records once existed but were destroyed in a fire, the date of which is unclear. In the building itself, bullet holes from revolutions or local skirmishes have been awkwardly patched, and plaster reapplied in places: evidence of periodic efforts to keep the place up. Inside, this same atmosphere of haphazard restoration speaks of local pride impeded by poverty and inexperience. Interior frescos are faded and chipped.

This place/moment/object is like a ghost in a land where the people themselves sometimes resemble ghosts. The Tarahumara or Rarámuri people are so poor that many reside in caves. In contrast with the museum-quality art produced by indigenous peoples in other parts of Mexico, their handicrafts are crude: little wooden stick dolls and small violins that sound scratchy and sad. These people's great claim to fame is running. Their cosmology is simple but profound. They speak of non-indigenous outsiders as "barking dogs" in reference to our chatter which they find superfluous and mostly meaningless.

At certain times of the year, the Tarahumara people hold their ancient ceremonies in the lost cathedral of Satevó. It seems good for the structure to have a reason to exist.

24

Ceramic Roof Bull, Peru

THIS CERAMIC BULL, a little more than a foot long and not quite a foot high at the span of its shoulders, is hollow with spout and handle. Yet using it as a receptacle of whatever sort would be secondary to its original purpose. In the high mountain areas of southern Peru, bulls such as these stand on the roof ridges of homes and other buildings. They often appear in sets of two, as if simulating a team of oxen. Frequently they support weather vanes and crosses or other symbols of Christianity—the syncretism so common throughout the indigenous world. I have also seen them adorned with coke bottles or similar relics of contemporary life.

The bulls are all about protection, keeping these buildings and their occupants safe, endowing them with long and prosperous lives. The roof bull tradition existed before the arrival of the Spanish. We know the Incas had something similar, although llamas took the place of bulls and small replicas of sun and moon predated the Christian trappings. It is believed that these adornments originally honored the Inca earth goddess Pachamama. The Incas also had statues of alpacas that they revered and believed brought good fortune. They called these *illas*. The figures had holes in their loins which they filled with alpaca fat, and they buried them in the earth so as to obtain healthy crops and a bountiful harvest.

My relationship to this bull is twofold. My parents bought it on a family trip to Peru in 1952. It speaks to me of childhood travels, adventures that surely sparked my ongoing curiosity about the world, her peoples and cultures. Having been in my parents' home until their deaths, it also represents one of the very few objects I inherited. My siblings and I were relaxed about what each wanted; there were no fights. My sister took Mother's jewelry and the copper pots she'd collected over the years. My brother got the oriental rugs and some of the heavy oak furniture, but scrupulously split with my sister and me what he got when he sold those pieces. I took little but memories and a couple of small objects, including this ceramic bull. Also a large plant, that I ultimately failed at keeping alive.

The bull sits in my studio. I like to believe it helps keep me safe.

25

Peruvian Weaving Spindle

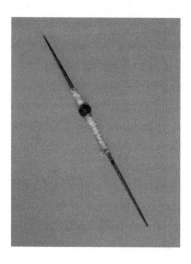

I CANNOT REMEMBER HOW I obtained this wooden spindle. I don't recall purchasing it or receiving it as a gift. I do know that it came into my possession in 1973–74, sometime during the months I worked in Peru. I'd been hired by the United Nations International Labor Office (ILO) to assist the Velasco Alvarado government in understanding the situation and needs of its country's women. In this capacity I traveled widely, interviewing city and country women, young and old, women whose first language was Quechua or Aymara, a broad range of voices. I learned a great deal and made my recommendations.

But the Velasco Alvarado administration was short-lived. After a few hopeful years, reactionary sectors forced the country back into its history of oppression and dependency. Velasco himself became ill, lost a leg and the presidency. The mid-seventies represented a dramatic moment in Latin America's story. A brutal coup had overthrown Salvador Allende's socialist revolution in Chile immediately to the south. Cuba, once more alone, struggled in the nearby Caribbean. Just a few years later, the Sandinistas would be victorious in Nicaragua, but their revolution—also short-lived—was then barely discernible on the horizon. Because it didn't fit any of the leftist molds—Maoist, Soviet-inspired, or influenced by Cuba—Velasco Alvarado's efforts in Peru have never received the attention they deserve.

This spindle clearly pretends to be "old," "authentic," a relic of another time. Because of its small size—it is only ten inches long—it may have been used by a child, one of the young girls who learn to weave from mother or grandmother. More probably, it was made to look old and sold to tourists as one of many items simulating a tool used in local weaving. I don't worry about it being authentic. Weaving, for me, has long been a metaphor for bringing together the diverse strands in the fabric of our lives. As I say, I have no memory of how this little spindle came into my possession. But I have carried it from home to home, country to country. There is something mysterious about it.

26

Woven Poncho, Cuzco, Peru

DURING THE MONTHS I worked in Peru, I spent quite a bit of time in the ancient highland city of Cuzco, a jumping-off spot for Machu Picchu, Sacsayhuamán, and other Inca ruins scattered across the Urubamba Valley. My work prevented me from visiting those sites at the time. Cuzco, back then, was the place from which I traveled to nearby villages, including 14,000-foot high Tinta, where centuries later, the women still wear black shoulder-length veils in mourning for their ancestral leader Tupac Amaru. I listened to their stories, tried to imagine their lives, and took notes for my report.

The altitude and cold affected me. Hotels didn't yet have oxygen available in their lobbies and, besides, I rarely stayed in a hotel. I sipped coca tea constantly and wrapped myself in this hand-woven poncho, similar to those worn by native women going about their business on Cuzco's stone streets.

Almost a half century later, this poncho remains one of my favorite articles of clothing but is packed away in an airtight container pungent with moth balls. When I travel to colder climates, where using it would be a comfort, I end up not taking it with me because it would fill an entire suitcase. During New Mexican winters, I invariably forget to put it on. Yet, when I began thinking about the 100 objects that define my life, this poncho was one of the first to come to mind. Its myriad threads span every color in that rugged region and its expert weaving is one of the oldest artforms known.

27

Saffron Strands

THOSE OF US WHO LOVE to cook are often obsessed with a particular herb or spice. My longtime favorite is saffron. I use it when making paella, a dish I began cultivating in the mid-1950s when living in southern Spain, or bouillabaisse, the sumptuous French seafood soup. Accessibly priced in Spain as well as in Afghanistan and other countries where the flower from which it comes is plentiful, in the United States, a pound goes for anywhere from $2,000 to $10,000 depending on quality—and on the willingness of the super-rich to spend that kind of money. This makes it the most expensive food on earth, worth more than truffles, caviar, or genuine balsamic vinegar. Fortunately, the small amount of saffron needed to flavor a paella or bouillabaisse can be purchased at most food markets for a price that, while high, is within reach of the middle-class shopper. I indulge in a small jar for very special occasions, and the scent of saffron-infused rice or fish stock filling a house is second only to that of freshly baked bread.

Saffron threads are the stamens of the crocus flower, a very high-maintenance plant that blooms for a single week out of the year. Each flower produces three stamens, which must be picked by hand and then delicately dried. One hundred fifty flowers and considerable labor are needed to produce a single gram of the spice. Some cooks, unable to afford the legitimate strands, substitute turmeric. There is no comparison—in scent, taste, or magic.

Deeply conscious of the gulf between rich and poor, I am someone who dresses simply, recoils—even when invited—from eating at an expensive restaurant, and detests ostentation of any kind. My love of saffron is an anomaly, then, one of several inexplicable desires that defy the rules by which I live my life.

28

Fake Mexican Passport

IN 1968, ALONG WITH hundreds of thousands of others, I took part in the Mexican student uprising. Such movements were common throughout the world that year: in Paris, New York, South Africa, and elsewhere. In most places, they eventually succumbed to governmental opposition, but managed to influence the political scene before they did so. In Mexico, opposition was particularly vicious, as the country was due to host the Summer Olympics on October 12th. Expensive sports installations and new hotels had been built and prospective visitors were beginning to cancel. Mexico's Gustavo Diaz Ordáz government came down hard on the movement, attacking a peaceful demonstration for five long hours with firepower from air and land. At Tlatelolco on October 2nd, 1968, as many as one thousand unarmed civilians may have died. The government claimed the toll had been twenty-six. The Olympic games went on as planned. The truth about the repression—news reports, photographs—was kept under wraps for thirty years.

In 1969, as the year anniversary of our movement approached, many of us hoped to honor our dead, exiled, or imprisoned comrades. We began making plans for memorial events. It was then that two plainclothes individuals came to my home and accused me of being a foreigner who operated a sweat shop without paying social security benefits to my employees. In fact, I wasn't a foreigner then. I had taken out Mexican citizenship two years earlier. Neither did I have a sweat shop or employees. I had recently given birth to my fourth child and had been ill since the delivery. I was in bed when those paramilitary men came to the house and Robert, my partner of those years, let them in. He told them that the information they had was wrong, and eagerly offered to prove my citizenship by showing them my Mexican passport.

A fatal mistake. One of the men, suddenly brandishing a gun, took the document, explaining he needed to fill out a form he had in his car. After they left, my partner raced upstairs, shouting: "They took your passport. They had a gun. They're gone!" I immediately reported the theft and applied for a replacement. A week later I was denied. Mexico's State Department falsely claimed I had lost three passports and such a situation needed to be investigated before it would issue me another. This began several months of trying to make my way out of Mexico to the safety of Cuba. We were forced to send our four children ahead, while investigating one dead end after another in my quest for a substitute document.

After many unsuccessful attempts, we were able to make contact with a friend who said he knew someone in the Mexican Mafia. For a price—$200—this man would get me a false passport that I could use for my escape. The plan involved my going to a beauty parlor in another part of the vast metropolis and claiming my husband was having an affair. I wanted a complete makeover, I said. Several hours later, I emerged from that salon, my long braid cut and teased, my hair dyed blue-black, and eyebrows tweezed into pencil-thin arches. A conventional navy blue and gold striped knit dress and lady's pumps and purse completed my disguise. With my new look, I stepped into one of those little shopping mall photo cubicles, opened my eyes wide, and obtained passport-sized pictures that showed a very different woman than the one I had been up to then. With those pictures in hand, we boarded a plane for the northern city of Chihuahua, where we were told our friend's contact would be waiting.

All went as planned until the following morning, when our contact took us to the local passport office where I expected to be able to buy the document I needed. The official who received us had clearly been informed of my situation. And he was delighted to help. But that's when everything began to unravel. That office didn't issue national passports, only a very different looking, pale blue accordion-like book used by people in that northern city who regularly needed to cross the border with the United States in order to work. For the document to be valid, it had to be registered at the Mexican consular office on the US side, something I couldn't risk. Faced with the need to make an on-the-spot decision, I said I'd take the useless book. Perhaps it would serve me in some way.

It never did. Robert took a bus to Ciudad Juárez and waited for us at a pre-arranged Chinese restaurant. Our contact meanwhile drove me to that border city in a refrigerated truck containing sides of beef. Just before the 28-mile checkpoint, he stopped the truck and I climbed in back with the meat. I couldn't make out the muffled conversation between my savior and the check point officer. Perhaps some money changed hands. A few miles later the truck stopped again, its driver released me from the cold and stench, and I climbed back into the cab to continue our journey at his side.

After a farewell dinner at the Chinese restaurant, our benefactor pointed us toward Friendship Bridge, and we walked into the United States. We answered the border guard's routine "Nationality?" with an equally routine "USA." I then took a Greyhound bus to the Canadian border, where I showed a copy of my birth certificate. In Toronto, I bought a ticket for Paris. No passport required to leave a country back then, only to enter one. In Paris, I boarded another flight for Prague, where Cuban contacts were waiting. Nineteen days later I was in Havana, reunited with my children. Robert, who had traveled legally from El Paso through New York and Madrid, had arrived the week before.

I never used this fake passport or border document. It turned out to be $200 worth of nothing. But I keep it as a reminder of those difficult times.

29

Deportation Hearing Papers

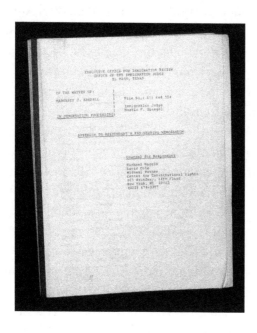

IN 1967, LIVING IN MEXICO and married to a Mexican, I took out Mexican citizenship. It wasn't a political act. I needed to be able to more easily find work in order to help support our family of five. Things became complicated when my Mexican passport was stolen at gun point in 1969. For the following twelve years, I lived as a person without a country. In 1980 I was finally able to get another legal Mexican passport, and in 1984 traveled with it to the United States where I hoped to regain my US citizenship and live peacefully in the land where I was born.

It wouldn't be that easy. Because I had lived in countries such as Cuba and Nicaragua, looked upon unfavorably by a succession of US administrations, and because of opinions expressed in some of my books, opinions contrary to US policy in Southeast Asia and Central America, I was denied an easy transition. After some months, I was ordered deported under the ideological exclusion clause of the 1952 McCarran-Walter Immigration and Nationality Act. I would have to wage an almost five-year battle to regain my citizenship.

My struggle began in El Paso, Texas, at an immigration hearing in March 1986. This appendix to respondent's pre-hearing memorandum is part of the voluminous paperwork coming from that hearing. I lost in El Paso and went on to other immigration courts, losing at each until I finally won in 1989 at the Court of Immigration Appeals in Washington DC. I have written extensively about this struggle that consumed me for so long and of the immense support for which I will always be grateful.[1]

More than thirty years have passed. Many objects remind me of those years in which I fought to come home in the legal as well as spiritual sense of that term. This packet of court papers is just one of them.

---

1. Most recently in my memoir, *I Never Left Home: Poet, Feminist, Revolutionary* (Durham: Duke University Press, 2020).

30

Nicole Hollander Cartoon

DURING THE YEARS OF my immigration struggle, many people came to my defense: writers, singer/song-writers, political and entertainment figures, family and friends. They sang for the case, participated in group poetry readings, hosted house parties and bowl-a-thons, took part in direct mailing campaigns. Nicole Hollander produced this cartoon which was printed as a postcard and sold to raise money. The references to Kurt Vonnegut, Norman Mailer and Alice Walker are because they, along with William Styron, Grace Paley, and Arthur Miller, brought a countersuit claiming that my deportation would deny them the right to interact with me. The original of this cartoon is framed and hangs in my studio.

31

Ancient Hand Tool, Uruguay

URUGUAY'S COASTLINE RUNS along the broad La Plata River all the way to Punta del Este, where river water mixes with the ocean. The river is so wide it resembles a sea. You can't see the other side, which is Argentina. West of the capital city of Montevideo, the tiny community of Kiyú is mostly a cluster of small cottages where people seek relief from summer heat. In the southern hemisphere the seasons are the opposite of ours; their summer is December through February.

My son and his family live in Uruguay. For years, they vacationed in a small fishing village called Santa Lucía del Este, where their grandparents' generation built a modest house and, with other leftists, helped improve the fishing families' lives. Now their summer home is in Maldonado, to the east of the capital. Almost Punta del Este, or Punta del Este without the ostentation. We have spent many happy days visiting them in both places. But when my daughter-in-law's father was alive, we sometimes went west to his tiny place at Kiyú. The beach wasn't immediately accessible like it is in the eastern fishing villages and resorts. Here, a steep clay cliff descends almost vertically to the water. From its exposed wall, storms sometimes reveal archeological finds: the bones of extinct animals, implements, and tools of peoples long disappeared from this place.

On one visit, my son spoke to me of a recent find, a large number of items that had emerged from the soft cliffside as if waiting to time-travel to now. He said those who'd made the discovery had tried to interest a museum in Montevideo, but the institution had replied they didn't have the room to house it. I was astonished when he added that the diggers had dozens of pieces at their home. "Where?" I asked. "Right across the way."

Within minutes, we were knocking on the neighbors' door. They welcomed us into their living room, which was filled, not with dozens, but hundreds of ancient implements of varying sizes. Bookshelves and coffee tables were spread thick. I asked if I could hold this almost featureless sphere. The man handed it to me, approximately an inch and a quarter in diameter. It fit perfectly in the cup of my hand, warming my flesh with a memory of centuries. I couldn't put it down.

And so we talked—about the area, the people who lived here so long ago, what each implement may have been used for. Perhaps this piece was one of three such stones attached to strings and launched by hand at prey that, once knocked to the ground, could be more easily captured. But the indentation worn by string is faint at best. Perhaps it wasn't a tool at all, but a meteorite; some who have seen it lean in that direction. I tend to think it was a tool, an instrument used to mash or pound other substances, maybe animal skins, bark, or food.

When it was time to go, I still held this small round stone in my palm. "Keep it," the woman of the house said, "as you can see, we have many more." My son began to protest, but I thanked her before anyone might convince her to retract the gift. I kept it in my pocket and, throughout the rest of our visit and on our flight home, often took it out to hold. Caress might be a better word. I felt and still feel that it carries a heat from a time long gone to this, the shape of a hand that labored a thousand years ago but is at home in mine.

32

Hand-Wrought Adz by Aurelio Falero, Uruguay

WE FIRST CAME UPON Aurelio Falero and his tools at Tristán Narvaja, the large Sunday flea market in the Cordón district of Montevideo. Among other stalls offering everything from fresh fruits to antiques, woven plastic shopping bags to ceramics, umbrellas and leather goods to kitchenware and keys that open nothing its buyer will ever possess, a stocky middle-aged man sips his mate surrounded by tools he fashions himself. He finds the well-used blades or axe heads in junkyards, then matches them to handles he carves from Uruguayan hardwoods. These are not ornamental. They are implements with faultless balance; an axe or hammer handle springs to the hand in one of two appropriate places. On handle or base, Falero affixes a brass band with his initials and the stylized image of a pig. Each perfectly assembled piece is a work of art.

Each time we visited Uruguay, we would go to Tristán Narvaja. And each time we went, we'd come back with a sample or two of Falero's handiwork. The man was always happy to welcome us. And he didn't tire of insisting we visit him at his home, in the small community called Tala in the department of Canelones. One day Barbara, my son, and I decided to try to find Falero's house.

We drove and drove. When we thought our destination might be near, we began asking if anyone knew where Falero lived. This was how we eventually arrived at a small, freshly whitewashed stone house fronted by a garden of immense sunflowers. We barely had time to get out of the car before Falero and his wife greeted us effusively. With some prodding, he showed us his workshop; he was embarrassed, he said, that it was so messy. An array of steel tools lay on makeshift worktables, their wooden handles in various stages of creation. Dozens of finished tools hung along one wall.

Falero and his wife lived in a series of small separate buildings: one a kitchen, another a bedroom, a third their living area. In a tiny restroom a modern toilet was as yet detached from plumbing. Their pristine garden overflowed with flowers. In a small fenced-off field were two sheep, beloved pets rather than simply providers of fine Uruguayan wool. The couple spoke with pride of their daughter and son, both at the university.

We marveled once again at the man's artistry, wondered how many of the world's artists live in poverty, making what they make simply because it's "what they feel compelled to do."

33

Piece of Berlin Wall

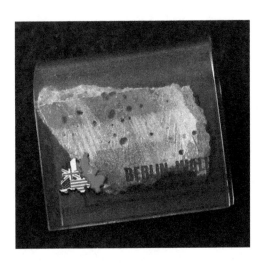

AS WITH "PIECES OF the true cross," there is always the possibility that some objects sold as pieces of the Berlin Wall may not be authentic. This one was given to me by a friend who lives in Berlin. I feel confident it is the real thing. It is encased in clear plastic, its signage in English for tourist consumption. It doesn't measure much more than an inch across.

Walls keep peoples out or in. They symbolize the terrible divisions of these times: between immigrants and locals, rich and poor, communities of different races, religions, needs. Autocratic governments want to erect more walls: keep the murderers and rapists away, they cry. As I write, Donald Trump continues to advocate for a solid "sea to sea" wall that is clearly a political ploy rather than anything remotely needed on our border with Mexico.

Some of these barriers, just in my lifetime, have been the 17th parallel dividing North and South Vietnam, the Berlin Wall, the demilitarized zone between North and South Korea, the wall between Israel and Palestine, the wall separating Ireland from Northern Ireland, the line between Cuba and the US-controlled Guantánamo Base, and that wall on our southern border that has become such an obsession for President Trump. Today, some countries in Western Europe hastily erect walls to keep out the floods of immigrants fleeing war-torn areas of Africa and the Middle East. Others open their door to these migrants, taking in as many as they can.

When the no-person's land between East and West that once ran through Berlin and much of Europe was opened up, it revealed a strip of land where birds sang among abundant vegetation. Not having been disturbed for decades, it held ecological surprises.

The first act in healing the world's wounds is tearing down the walls.

34

Vietnamese Water Puppet

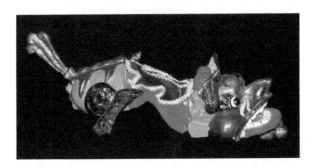

IN 1974, I TRAVELED to North Vietnam and to the liberated territory of Quang Tri, just below the 17th Parallel. The country was still divided, the war in the south still raged. I was living in Cuba at the time and, along with my regular job, volunteered to give weekly English lessons to the man who headed The Voice of Vietnam.[1] I had written a book about Cuban women, and the Vietnamese wanted me to write about their heroic women, many of whom were shouldering the brunt of the struggle. The North Vietnamese Women's Union invited me to visit their country, travel its length, interview its women. They hoped I would write about them.[2] It was an unforgettable

---

1. A short-wave radio broadcast aimed at US listeners and repeated several times daily, which the Cubans provided to the Vietnamese during the war.

2. *Spirit of the People: Vietnamese Women Two Years from the Geneva Accords* (Vancouver, New Star Books, 1975). *El espíritu de un pueblo*

experience. I was told I was one of only nine foreigners in North Vietnam at the time.

Twenty-eight years later, Barbara and I traveled as tourists to a unified Vietnam. My earlier visit had been a work trip, not one that gave itself to shopping or attending cultural events. This time around, I soaked up the country's rich culture and art: theater, music, puppet shows, museums, even the underground tunnels where the Vietcong had established schools, factories, and operating theaters beneath US bases during the war.

I bought this puppet after an evening at Hanoi's famous Water Puppet Theater.

---

is the Spanish language edition published by Siglo XXI, Editores, SA, Mexico City, also in 1975.

35

Red Lacquer Doors,
Temple of Literature, Hanoi

VISITING VIETNAM IN peacetime, I could delight in its millennial treasures, love of the arts, architectural gems. Now, when I think of Hanoi, I remember these lacquered doors rather than the manholes that once dotted that city's streets and served as entrances to individual bomb shelters in the event of US air strikes.

Vietnam has had to fight as much as any country on earth, for more than 2,000 years, just to enjoy the independence and peace reflected in its stoic people's lives.[1]

---

1. The first Chinese conquest of Vietnam dates to 111 BC. Since then, the peninsula has had to fight off domination by the Chinese, French, and finally Americans.

36

Ho Chi Minh Medal

I NEVER WEAR IT. Doing so would seem out of place, ostentatious. And who, among my friends today, would even recognize the likeness of the beloved Vietnamese leader?[1] Yet I am deeply proud of it.

I was given this medal in 1975, after the Vietnamese patriots had defeated the United States and reunified their

---

1. Ho Chi Minh was born Nguyen Sinh Cung in 1890, in a village in central Vietnam that was then part of French Indochina. Uncle Ho, as he was later called, worked as a cook and other jobs as a young man. He was influenced by the Russian Revolution, founded the Indochinese Communist Party in 1930 and the League for the In-dependence of Vietnam in 1941. He was frequently imprisoned for his political activism. At the end of World War II, Viet Minh forces seized the city of Hanoi and declared a democratic state in the north. Ho became its president, a position he held until his death in 1969.

nation. It was placed around my neck by comrades at the North Vietnamese Embassy in Havana. I wasn't the only one to receive this example of their gratitude; many of us, ashamed of our country's war of aggression, had done what we could: small tasks such as writing, translating, teaching English. We never expected anything in return.

I was in Prague in 1969 when Ho Chi Minh died. I remember seeing photographs in newspapers and magazines of long lines of Vietnamese crying inconsolably. Years later, when Barbara and I visited Vietnam as tourists, we visited Ho Chi Minh's home: a simple two-room structure, impressive in its austerity. We also lined up with hundreds to enter the mausoleum where his embalmed body is preserved in a glass coffin. I am generally not attracted to such displays and couldn't have imagined the overwhelming emotion I felt.

37

Banana Flower, Vietnam

I CAN'T REMEMBER WHERE I photographed this banana flower. Somewhere in Vietnam. An image that represents a moment of blooming, a moment as tenuous and fleeting as any.

What can be said of a flower? Perhaps the wisest was what The Little Prince said about his: "If a person loves a flower that is the only one of its kind on all the millions and millions of stars, then gazing at the night sky is enough to make him happy."[1]

---

1. *The Little Prince* is a novella written by French aristocrat, poet, and pioneering aviator Antoine de Saint-Exupéry. It first appeared in 1943, has been translated into 300 languages and dialects, and has sold 140 million copies world-wide, making it one of the most popular books of all time.

38

The Joy of Cooking

IT'S THE COOKBOOK EVERY American woman of my generation has in her kitchen. Every woman, that is, who likes to cook and depends on cookbooks for the finer details. Like Benjamin Spock's *Baby and Child Care*, Irma and Marion Rombauer's *Joy of Cooking* has enjoyed dozens of editions, each one incorporating new ideas about food preparation. I can't remember when this 75th anniversary edition replaced my original version. Cooking with a surplus of butter gave way to eating healthier fare, but the old standbys are still there.

39

My Clay Bread Molds

I BEGAN BAKING BREAD when I returned to the United States in 1984 and had the luxury of a working oven. Buttermilk, rye, raisin and nut, pumpernickel, whole wheat, cornmeal, French baguettes, and more. They require different pans, but these clay molds are my favorites. Their porous inner surfaces have never received the insult of soap; wiping them clean insures they will always exude nothing but the scent of freshly baked dough.

40

Lumi Videla Tapestry, Chile

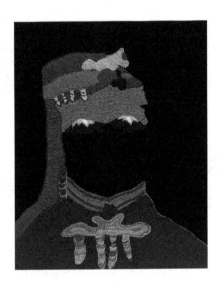

IT WAS 1975, and I was on a lecture tour across Canada, speaking about Cuban women. But Chilean women and men were also very much on my mind. Not much more than a year before, Augusto Pinochet's 1973 coup had toppled that country's socialist revolution, leaving Salvador Allende and hundreds of other Chileans dead. Thousands more had been disappeared or were being tortured in prisons and secret detention camps. The fortunate had managed to find refuge, most in Europe or Canada.

When I arrived in the small city of Fredericton, New Brunswick, my first event of the day was a small gathering at the local women's bookstore. Among the twenty or so women who attended, I noticed one from Chile. Her name was Coca Milán. She told me that she and her husband had been exiled to this small town, most of whose inhabitants didn't even know where Chile was. They had been warmly welcomed, but it was a lonely exile.

We talked about what was happening back home. Coca mentioned she'd been a member of the Movement of the Chilean Left (MIR, in its Spanish acronym). I happened to be working in Cuba with members of that organization, collecting testimonies of women who'd survived the coup and its aftermath of torture.

It was my birthday, December 6th. That night, I spoke at the city's university, a larger venue. Coca came back, bringing her husband. She also brought something else. It was a tapestry she'd made in honor of Lumi Videla, a member of the MIR's leadership who had died in the dictatorship's torture chambers. Somehow the prisoner had gotten ahold of a razor blade and, as her torturer raped her, she tried to cut his throat. He overpowered her. She didn't stand a chance. The dictatorship tossed Lumi's body over a wall into the Italian Embassy garden. By doing so, they hoped to create friction between members of the MIR and Communists, both of whom had sought asylum there. All they created was deeper solidarity. When Coca discovered it was my birthday, she handed me the tapestry. "I want you to have it," she said.

I was stunned. I hadn't known Lumi Videla, but several of my informants had told me about the brilliant young woman who was now another number among those whose lives had been snuffed out by the fascist coup. I

knew she'd been partial to indigenous outfits with Mapuche motifs. As I looked at Coca's tapestry, I recognized
the Mapuche blouse and colored yarn in Lumi's braid,
the way the cordillera that rises above Santiago becomes
her eyes.

When I returned to Cuba with this tapestry, my Chilean friends recognized Lumi too. The abstract likeness was
perfect, they said. I framed it and it's hung in my home ever
since, moving with me from Cuba to Nicaragua and from
Nicaragua back to the United States. In 1992, West End
Press published a collection of my poems called *Dancing
with the Doe*. We reproduced the tapestry on the cover. I
often wonder where Coca Milán is today, perhaps back in
her native Chile. Her gift continues to remind me of the
fighting spirit of women everywhere.

THE UNBURIED, THE MISSING

come back to me now. Roque, months older than I
when we started out, forever forty.
Doris María, who would not become a teen.
The plane that took her falls from the sky,
falls again each time I turn my eyes to hers:
round in their fear of fire. Nothing will happen next.
María Otilia Vargas, seventy-five-year-old retired teacher,
widow of Osvaldo Pérez, mother of
Dagoberto, Aldo, Carlos, Iván, Mireya and Patricia,
the first gunned down in a fire fight against the dictator,
next two extinguished in that long war's torture cells
and the twins still missing, "disappeared"
in that language of Chilean pain. Only Patricia

lives, each of her years unraveling to the next,
accompanying her mother's purpose
in sweet madness. Together they study each release
on a list published all this time too late.
Their beloved names aren't there
yet the mother continues to tempt them
with rice pudding,
shelter their bodies from night air,
cradle them against her hopeful breast.
Otilia, condemned
to live these years her children could not have.
Even Patricia has lost count: the sister and brothers
torn from her childhood murmur in her ear.
The missing will only come back to us
when we set a table
served with the food of change.[1]

1. *Where They Left You for Dead / Halfway Home* (Boulder: EdgeWork Books, 2002), 71–72.

41

Pueblo del Arroyo, Chaco Canyon, New Mexico

CHACO, A COMPLEX OF what we call great houses in a broad canyon northwest of Española, New Mexico, is believed to have been the center of the Ancestral Puebloan world. Between 850 and 1150 AD, the site was a major cultural and ceremonial hub for the peoples who lived in the region. Some two hundred outlier communities were linked to Chaco by broad avenues now visible only from the sky. Some of these avenues were nine meters across, much wider than what would have been needed for ordinary transport. Anthropologists believe this extreme width signaled ceremonial use, rather than merely transit.

Chacoans quarried sandstone blocks and hauled timber from great distances, building fifteen major complexes that were the largest buildings in North America until the 19th century. Their stonework is unique and impressive. One of the great houses, Pueblo Bonito, had more than six hundred rooms and a dozen round underground pits called kivas. Many of the buildings at Chaco were aligned to capture the solar and lunar cycles, and there is evidence that complex archeoastronomy was practiced there. Today, at solstice and equinox, people come from great distances to celebrate these astronomical features. A fifty-year drought, beginning in 1130, is thought to have led to the site's eventual abandonment.

Exposed and extremely hot in the summer, the best time to visit Chaco is spring and fall. When I was a child, one had to take a long deeply rutted road north from old Route 66, now I-40. Getting there took seven hours or more. Depending on conditions, there was a good chance of getting stuck. I remember one excursion on which we never reached the ruin; my father drove our station wagon into a ditch. A Navajo man happened along with a wagon and horses and managed to pull us out. By that time, it was late afternoon and we headed home.

Today one drives north past Española and west on sixteen miles of dirt road that is usually kept in passable condition. The trip from Albuquerque is a little more than two hours. A visitor center and campground are the only facilities. There is no place to buy food. Those of us who love Chaco don't really want greater accessibility or additional facilities. We live close to the center of the world and want to keep it as unaltered as possible.

Chaco can be both thrilling and frightening. There are those who feel powerful vibes in some parts of the site, evidence that torture and other painful acts were perpetrated there. In other areas one can wander peacefully, crouching to pass through low, keyhole-shaped doorways and enter rooms whose masonry still astonishes. Few visitors arrive on any given day. Contemplation and wonder are undisturbed. In the past few years, the area is threatened by oil extraction, and those of us who love Chaco hope we can prevent fracking, which would very certainly negatively affect the site.

> [...] At Chaco's northernmost reach
> two towers,
> each catching moonrise
> in the perfect balance
> of its slender notch.
> Astronomical alignments
> speaking to future.
> Once every 18.6 years
> the lunar standstill
> cycles from Pueblo Bonito's priests
> to our forced double take.[1]

---

1. Fragment of "Time," in *Stones Witness* (Tucson: University of Arizona Press, 2007), 56.

42

Turquoise Bead, Chaco

IT WAS A HOT, DRY, late summer afternoon. We were walking along the base of the cliff that runs from Pueblo Bonito to Chetro Ketl, two of Chaco's great houses. I looked down and, less than an inch from my right toe was a tiny turquoise bead. Smaller than a half centimeter in diameter, a perfect hole had been carved in its center; once it must have been strung with other beads in a necklace or bracelet. There is spiral striation visible around the circumference of the bead, more prominent on one side than the other.

I picked up the bead and held it my hand. I closed my fingers around it and images of Chacoan women adorned with turquoise and shells exploded behind my eyes. "You know you have to put it back," Barbara said. I nodded in agreement but did nothing. When we left Chaco that day, the bead was in my Levi pocket. Years have passed. I've considered returning it to the powdery sand where I found it, but never have. I know the rules: no artifacts or even stones must be taken from ancient sites.

I cannot bring myself to part with this bead, which whispers its stories in my ear.

43

Stone Fountain by Joshua Gannon, Madrid, New Mexico

WHEN WE MOVED FROM the foothills east of Albuquerque to a smaller house in the city, we had a proper
backyard for the first time. The Southwestern United
States has been conscious of the value of water more palpably, perhaps, than other parts of the nation, and our
home already had what they call xeriscape landscaping,
a lawn style increasingly popular in these parts: a spread
of pebbles instead of grass, a few hardy trees, native plants
that need little moisture to survive.

Desert landscapes and water are little understood by
those who haven't experienced the ways in which they

impact each other. Popular desert images include death from dehydration, lack of the life-sustaining substance. But more people drown on deserts than die from lack of water. A thunderstorm many miles away can send a flash flood crashing through a narrow canyon, destroying everything in its path. Almost every year, groups of hikers are caught in fatal situations from which they cannot escape.

Soon after our move, we found this fountain in the village of Madrid. It recycles a small amount of water, and thus combines efforts to save the precious liquid with an aura of lushness. Joshua Gannon carves his rock fountains from a local quarry. When he came to install ours, he surrounded the base with river stones. The gentle gurgling of water in summer attracts roadrunners and other birds.

The sound of water is its own language.

44

Cuban Flag and Santería Tool Necklace

I LIVED IN CUBA from 1969 through 1980. I think of that period as the Revolution's glory years, when promise seemed unblemished, justice achievable, and the vast majority of citizens worked enthusiastically for change. We were confident we were building a better world. And that we would prevail.

The flag is a patriotic symbol, the Santería necklace representative of the African religions which, back then, were looked upon as conflicting with Marxist ideology. By placing these objects together, I am speaking of the complexity that is always present when enduring social change is the goal.

Things are rarely only what they seem.

45

Martín's Dog Tag, Angola

IN 1975 AGOSTINHO NETO, the revolutionary president of Angola, asked Cuba for military help routing CIA-backed forces determined to defeat his socialist government. Fidel Castro spoke before a million people in Havana's Plaza of the Revolution. He traced the history of African slaves kidnapped from their homelands and brought to Cuba to work the sugar plantations. Cuba has a long debt with Africa, he said, and it was only fitting that Cubans should return to Africa to help defend nations that had given so much to the Island: "We are not only a Latin American nation; we are also a Latin African nation [...] African blood runs abundant in our veins. From Africa, many of our ancestors came to this land as slaves

[...] We are brothers and sisters of the Africans and for the Africans we are ready to fight!"[1]

Over the next several years, thousands of Cubans went to fight in Angola and Namibia. Their efforts made the difference. Not only did they succeed in helping to free those countries; they also helped defeat apartheid in South Africa. Despite the deplorable conditions, risk, and sacrifice, people wanted to join the internationalist forces. Those deemed physically or psychologically unfit resented not being allowed to go. Following the military campaign, thousands of Cuban doctors and other technicians worked two-year stints in Africa and in developing countries throughout the world, offering their expertise to peoples who lacked almost everything. Revolutionary Cuba's internationalism has been extraordinary.[2]

My friend Martín is a sociologist. He completed two tours in Angola, the first in a military capacity, the second as a government consultant. When he returned, he gave me his dog tag. I keep it as a kind of talisman of commitment in a world ever more given to profit and greed.

---

1. Fidel Castro, December 22, 1975. Translation MR.
2. I wrote a book about Cuban internationalism, *Exporting Revolution: Cuba's Global Solidarity* (Durham: Duke University Press, 2017).

46

Casa de las Américas, Havana, Cuba

ON THE OUTSIDE, it seems an ordinary building: small, gray, with modest art nouveau lines, its paint in places suffering the effects of saltwater damage. Sitting at the bottom of broad Avenida de los Presidentes in Vedado, just across from Havana's *malecón*, storm surges often bring sudden waves lapping dangerously at its door. Its three floors are a modest combination of lecture halls, galleries, a small bookstore, and offices. Ever-changing art exhibitions grace the walls. For those of us who have a long history with Casa de las Américas, this is a space where Revolution lives, Revolution with a capital R.

Early in 1959, just months after Cuba's rebel army had forced a rabid dictator from power, Fidel Castro tapped Haydée Santamaría to head an institution he hoped would be able to break through the cultural blockade. He foresaw US intervention and knew that the cultural arena would be as important as the economic, military, or diplomatic in fighting for Cuba's right to exist on its own terms.

Haydée, who'd grown up on a sugar plantation in the central part of the country and who hadn't been able to study past sixth grade in a one-room schoolhouse, had been one of only two women who'd participated in the Revolution's initial military action. Surviving it, she'd served time in prison. Then she'd gone on to take part in every aspect of the struggle: the city underground, the war in the mountains, and clandestine trips to the United States to buy weaponry. She was fearless and creative, deeply Cuban and, most of all, innately brilliant.

At that first military action, the rebels had lost. The regime vowed it would kill ten revolutionaries for every soldier shot. Haydée's brother and lover were both tortured to death. Gloating officers had presented her with her brother's eyes and lover's testicles to try to get her to reveal Fidel's whereabouts. She refused, but the experience took its toll. Perhaps her ability to function while besieged by ghosts was one of the attributes that enabled her to understand artistic sensibility. Haydée drew to Casa the great artists and intellectuals of several generations as the flower draws bees. Soon Jean-Paul Sartre, Simone de Beauvoir, Gabriel García Márquez, Julio Cortázar, Laurette Sejourné, Violeta Parra, Ernesto Cardenal, and others were frequent visitors. She became their friend, confidant, someone who could explain the Revolution to them in a way that made sense.

But Haydée also created an institution based on democratic principles, horizontal power-sharing, equality, and pride. She had unflinching ideas about how people work best together. She was a feminist before that word entered the Spanish lexicon. From her respected leadership position, she consistently struggled so that the Revolution's stated ideals were put into practice. She provided an unparalleled example of fairness. During repressive periods, she knew how to pull in and fly below the radar. But she never stopped embracing difference. When brilliant artists were being harassed because they were queer or otherwise "different," she made a place for them at Casa.

Almost forty years after Haydée Santamaría's death, Casa de las Américas remains a place of unwavering revolutionary practice. Creativity and change. Risk and a recognition of what is forward-looking, vital, important. Respect for and love of the arts in all their manifestations. I have returned many times. Walking through Casa's door, I am embraced by Haydée's spirit, still at the institution's heart.

47

Gregory's Puppet, Cuba

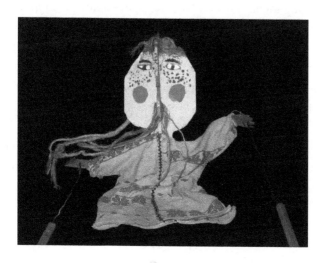

AFTER I WAS HIT BY Mexican governmental repression in the summer of 1969, I had to lay low while trying to find my way out of the country. We sent our four children—eight, five, four years, and three months old—on ahead to Cuba, where we knew they would be cared for until we could join them. It was a difficult time, plagued by danger and risk, loneliness and uncertainty, illness and finally relief at being together again. We reunited in Havana in October and lived at the Hotel Caprí for several months until assigned the apartment we would live in for the next eleven years.

Gregory was always curious about his surroundings, proactive in finding interesting places to go, things to do.

The Caprí was right around the corner from Cuba's National Puppet Theater and it wasn't long before my son began visiting its workshop. He fashioned this puppet from the wood and repurposed nails that had once been a box holding the famous Cuban cigars; the hotel gift shop sold many such boxes. In Cuba's atmosphere of scarcity, Gregory scoured the streets for rope to make his puppet's hair, coat-hanger wire for the rods that allowed its movement, paint for the features of the face. The puppet's outfit is cut from a dress outworn by his baby sister, Ana.

I have kept this puppet almost half a century. It is coated with the grime of places and situations, weather and moves. Each time I look at it I am reminded of the wonder of a child's imagination, creativity unleashed even in the most restrictive circumstances.

48

Girl with Plastic Shoes, Havana

DURING MY YEARS IN Mexico, Cuba, and Nicaragua, I continued to write poetry in English. I spoke Spanish but could never manage to bring that language to the level of what I needed to express myself poetically. As a result, there was a gulf between my artist self and my closest friends and contemporaries. I couldn't even share my poems with my children. This disjuncture may have been partly responsible for my desire to learn photography: a creative language that didn't depend on words. The more immediate reason was simply that I felt frustrated by the photographs taken by those professionals assigned to accompany me when I did cultural journalism for Cuban publications. I often found myself wanting to ask: "Why don't you shoot that?" or "Don't you notice what's happening over there?" But respect for their own artistic choices made me hesitant to do so.

In 1978, I apprenticed to a fine Cuban photographer named Ramón Martínez Grandal.[1] We called him Grandal. He was aggressive and sensitive, his blustering exterior covering an inner gentleness. Our apartment had a tiny, unused, and forlorn servant's bathroom left over from a pre-revolutionary time when domestic service was a feature of middle-class life. It didn't have a door, so we hung an old sheet and worked between eleven at night and dawn when the city lights were dim and our ninth floor was mostly shrouded in shadow. The cubicle no longer had running water, so we washed our prints in the nearby stone tub where we also did our laundry. In the Cuba of those years, there were no stores where you could buy packets of powders you could mix with water to produce developer, stop bath, or fixer. We mixed our own from the chemicals we'd get at compound pharmacies—when we could get them.

Grandal was a wonderful teacher and I learned quickly. Coming to photography at that stage in my life—I was in my early forties by then—I had developed an artistic sensibility but lacked the technical knowhow required by this new craft. I had to learn chemistry to progress. Film and paper were also scarce. We got the former from the Cuban film industry, where a friend gave us the unused ends from newsreel stock. We begged the latter from friends visiting from the US or Europe.

---

1. Ramón Martínez Grandal, 1950–2017.

Sometimes, I would work late at night and spread my prints out on our large dining room table for Grandal to critique when he dropped by the following day. This image of the young girl with a pile of plastic shoes at the bottom of the stairwell in a housing project east of the city was the first of which I was proud. It has what I love most in a photograph, the seen and unseen: the girl on whom I focused and the little boy walking behind her who I didn't notice until I took the print from the developing tray. This early picture is still one of my favorites.

49

Grand Canyon, Arizona

THE GRAND CANYON OF the Colorado River is one of the world's wonders, at once vast and intimate, awe-inspiring in every season, impossible to describe in either words or images to those who have not stood on its rim or descended its depths. I visited Grand Canyon for the first time with my parents and siblings when I was ten years old. Living only seven hours away, I've been there dozens of times since. Three times, Barbara and I have run its 286 miles of raging river in wooden dories. We have entered it by mule and on foot. I overcame severe vertigo and fear of heights in order to be able to brave its trails.

Barbara and I collaborated on a book of poems and drawings that emerged after one of those river runs.[1] The

---

1. *Into Another Time: Grand Canyon Reflections* (Albuquerque: West End Press, 2004).

poems are rich with geological data and a magnified sense of time. The drawings, among the few I've seen of the Canyon that don't depend on color, trace perspective in black and white lines of pen and ink.

Grand Canyon is definitely our special place. No matter how many thousands of other visitors we must share it with, we are always there alone. We have taken children, grandchildren, and close friends to experience its wonders. An especially intense visit was just after Barbara and I got together; the architect of Canyon structures, Mary Elizabeth Jane Colter, visited me in a dream and told me we'd find the rings we wanted at one of its shops. Another especially meaningful trip was with María Vázquez Valdez, my friend and translator who rendered *Into Another Time* into Spanish.

I've probably made more than a thousand photographs of Grand Canyon. None do it justice, but this one comes closest.

DEER CREEK I

Where this river moves
against its wall of schist
one point seven billion years
unfold.
That seam gives
movement to magnitude,
spirit to body,
place to time.
Colors hold stories
just as my heart
in its slowing rhythm

beats against your lips.
High above
where Paiute handprints
fade on the Tapeats wall
their movement of transformation
brings my hands softer, closer,
another river
superimposed upon this one
closing its fingers
over my own.[2]

2. *Into Another Time: Grand Canyon Reflections*, 41.

50

Hermit's Rest, Grand Canyon

MARY ELIZABETH JANE COLTER (1869–1958) was
an architect when few women in the United States held
such credentials. She didn't formally hold them either,
but Fred Harvey of railway fame discovered her and was
impressed by her talent. He hired her to design his railroad depot hotels, and her buildings soon placed her in
the pantheon of great American builders. She used native
materials before Frank Lloyd Wright, although he never
acknowledged her influence. She brought attention to
Native artists by using their art in her buildings. It took
decades, however, for her work to be considered worthy
of serious study. Workmen often resented laboring under

a woman, especially when she demanded they haul heavy rocks long distances to build her signature fireplaces.

Many of Colter's great hotels have been lost, torn down in the 1970s when air travel replaced trains. One, La Posada in Winslow, Arizona, managed to escape destruction and has been renovated to simulate the original. A half dozen of her buildings still stand on the south rim of Grand Canyon, and Phantom Ranch in the Canyon's depths is also hers.

On my 61st birthday, Barbara, our friend Jane Norling, and I made a pilgrimage to all of Colter's Grand Canyon structures. Hermit's Rest, at the end of the west rim drive, might be my favorite.

51

Mary Elizabeth Jane Colter Place Setting (replica)

MARY ELIZABETH JANE COLTER was a designer as well as an architect. She created the beautiful tableware for the Santa Fe Chief's dining car, bringing stylized Mimbres motifs and elegance to what was once the most luxurious way to travel cross-country. Colter's original dishes, flatware, and glasses are now in museums. But replicas have been fabricated over the years. Barbara and I first saw these copies at La Posada in Winslow. We bought a couple of place settings on our 15th anniversary and added to our collection each year until we owned a service for twelve. I used to take out these plates and glasses only on special occasions. Then I started using them every time friends came to dinner. I never miss an opportunity to tell people about Colter, her talent and persistence in a male world.

52

Pentax K1000 Camera

THIS WAS MY FIRST camera, or a picture of what it looked like. I was living in Cuba, had apprenticed to a Cuban photographer and would soon move to Nicaragua, where I intuited I would need a sturdy serviceable model immune to bumpy roads and other harsh conditions. The K1000 served me well, but when the Contra war exploded, I graduated to Pentax's more advanced L series. It had a motor that made it more appropriate for shooting in rapidly changing situations.

I used a film camera, developing and printing my own pictures until many years later, when emphysema forced me out of the dark room. Then, like so many photographers of my generation, I moved on to a digital camera, substituting Photoshop for hands-on darkroom work. Now, with a slight tremor that's come with age, I've had to stop making pictures altogether. I still miss the film camera and darkroom.

53

Dougga, Tunisia

WE VISITED TUNISIA IN spring 2011, just a few months after that country was the first to launch the Arab Spring. In the capital, Tunis, barbed wire and tanks still lined the streets, evidence of continuing struggle. One evening, people suddenly filled the area around our hotel, demanding recent conquests be honored. It was exciting to be able to spend time in a country where change had been so recent, and everyone was willing to share opinions about what had happened and what they hoped the outcome would be.

Dougga was a settlement of Berber and Roman origin founded in the 6th century BC. Located in the midst of gentle countryside, it has been protected from modern urbanization, in contrast with other important ruins such as Carthage, which has been pillaged and rebuilt many times over. At Dougga, Numidian, Berber, Punic, ancient Roman, and Byzantine histories converge. Well-preserved buildings stand in all their glory. The stonework is unusually fine and very beautiful. A few mosaic floors are still visible, although the site's most important mosaics have been moved for safekeeping, some to the Bardo Museum in Tunis. Temples, a theater, baths, and other structures evoke a time when they were the scenes of vibrant city life.

As is true of other objects or places in this book, what I most treasure from Dougga isn't visible in the photograph. It's a large sundial-like feature called Rose of the Winds. Faded by time and weather and impossible to capture in a photograph, it remains engraved only in my memory. Its mystery, hidden in this picture like the Little Prince's elephant is hidden in his drawing of a boa constrictor, is poetry in its subtlest form.

54

Poet of Two Hemispheres Prize, Quito, Ecuador

WHEN I RECEIVED AN invitation to the 11th Poesía en Paralelo Cero (Poetry at the Equator), a yearly poetry festival held in Quito, Ecuador, I accepted with pleasure. I knew I would be spending a week among Latin American poets, many of them friends or acquaintances. I knew it would be exciting to experience Ecuador's version of what a gathering of poets can be. But I couldn't have imagined the surprises ahead.

I got wind of the first of those surprises when, a couple of weeks before traveling, the festival organizer, Xavier

Oquendo Troncoso, wrote asking if I would accept its highest honor, the "Poet of Two Hemispheres" prize. Three poets have previously received this award: the Argentinean Juan Gelman in 2013, the Spanish/Philippine singer-songwriter Luis Eduardo Aute in 2016, and in 2017, Antonio Gamoneda of Spain. I consider Juan Gelman to be one of the greatest poets of my generation; any honor previously given to him has special meaning for me. It also pleased me immensely to be the first woman awarded this prize. Of course, I accepted joyously.

When I arrived in Quito, another surprise awaited. El Angel Editores, also directed by Oquendo, had published an anthology of my poetry in Spanish. My dear friends Víctor Rodríguez Núñez and Katherine M. Hedeen had made the selection, translated much of the work, and written a prologue without letting me know what was going on. The beautiful edition appeared in El Angel's "Monstruos" series, an imprint which publishes books by poets the publisher considers particularly important. Oquendo, who met my plane, handed me a copy of *Lenguaje del Tiempo* before we'd exited the airport parking lot. I was thrilled to see they'd used a drawing by Barbara on the cover.

One of the unique aspects of this week-long festival is its presence throughout the country. Most such gatherings take place in a single city. Here, seventy-five poets from Cuba, Colombia, Chile, Mexico, Spain, Greece, Russia, Ecuador, and the United States (I was the sole US poet) spent a few days in Quito and then separated into smaller groups to read and participate in local activities in a dozen other places. I went to Guayaquil, where the newly established University of the Arts had a full program planned, and Esmeraldas on the northwestern coast, where its vibrant black culture captivated those of us willing to make the six-hour bus trip from mist-shrouded highlands to tropical heat. Others visited Cuenca, Ambato, Otavalo, Machachi, Lacunga, Tulcán, Ibarra, Ríobamba, and Ipiales. We performed in schools and universities, presented books, talked about translation, read our own poems, listened to one another, and just hung out—sharing books, stories, and memories. It was an exuberant week of poetry, close comradeship, and meaningful conversation.

For me, the most moving event was the festival's inauguration, held at Quito's imposing Capitol Theater. That's when the awards were given, mine and three others honoring Chilean Omar Lara, Cuban Nancy Morejón, and Ecuadorean Violeta Luna. When Xavier handed me the stone statue, I thought I recognized its style. I later confirmed that it was carved by my old friend, the sculptor and poet Sara Palacios. I was overcome with emotion and almost speechless as I took it in my hands.

A prelude to the awards ceremony was the showing of a marvelous film of Jorgenrique Adoum reading his poem "Se prohibe fijar carteles (Putting Up Posters is Forbidden)." Watching and listening to Jorgenrique read in the apartment where sixteen years ago, Barbara and I had dinner with him and his wife Nicole, filled me with nostalgia. So many of my generation's great poets are gone now.

As he handed me the statue, Xavier Oquendo said: "Margaret, you have had a dignified presence in all the events that have figured in our Latin American history: the Cuban and Sandinista revolutions, the Vietnam and Cold Wars, the Beat generation in the United States, which, by breaking with the academic canon, has had such an impact on our own poetic language. You have lived at a time when poets were intellectuals occupying the trenches in place and word, struggling against the status quo (…) Beyond all that, you fueled the change in what we call the greater Spanish nation. The Spanish language owes you a great deal. Your work as editor of *El Corno Emplumado* is iconic in the history of poetry in our languages (…) For this reason, Paralelo Cero now awards the most important honor it gives a poet, The Prize of Two Hemispheres, to a woman who has contributed with her voice, body, and heart to building a better world—in favor of the word even when taking that position was painful."

I felt immensely humbled by this attention to my life and work.

I wanted to give something back at Poesía en Paralelo Cero 2019 and decided I would read my poetry directly in Spanish. For many years I had been reading in English—the language in which I write—with a translator at my side following each poem with its Spanish version. Enough, I thought. It's time I make the effort, when in Latin America, to read in the language of my audiences. And so, I did.

55

Oak Tree House, Mesa Verde, Colorado

ATOP A HIGH PLATEAU in southern Colorado, Mesa Verde's canyons and ancient dwellings are spread across the two long arms of this Ancestral Puebloan site. People we now call Paleo Indians first wandered and maybe stayed here for short periods as long ago as 7500 BC. Permanent settlements established themselves around 650 BC, and people began constructing the massive cliff dwellings, many of them several stories high, at the end of the 12th century AD. By 1285, following a period of environmental and perhaps also social instability, the people abandoned the mesa and moved south into what is now Arizona and New Mexico. Tens of thousands of people a year visit Mesa Verde, hike into its ruins, transporting themselves into a world that is palpably present and that speaks to us from the past.

The foregoing is general data. But Mesa Verde is personal for me. We live a mere five and a half hours away. When Barbara and I were first together and times were much leaner than they are now, we used to put our combined loose change in a large coffee can each night and save until we had $150. That amount covered a trip to Mesa Verde: gas, food, a couple of nights in a hotel, everything. We would drive north from Albuquerque on any long weekend, begin getting excited as soon as we spotted the mesa, turn off and begin making our way up along the switchback road that climbs to its top. We'd often see wild turkey and deer before arriving at Farview, the Park's only hotel.

Farview has no TVs or even telephones in the rooms. The idea: stop worrying about your everyday concerns, connect with where you are. Each room has a small terrace. You can sit on it and gaze into a valley whose silhouetted ridges recede in purple-blue haze as evening falls. I was once startled to see a black bear in the distance, standing on its hind legs. On clear days, you can make out the tip of Shiprock, far off on Navajo land.

The summer Mesa Vista celebrated one hundred years as a National Park, the administration offered a couple of special hikes to Mug and Oak Tree houses, ruins that were made accessible only on that occasion. I immediately signed us up for both. Oak Tree was especially magical. We were less than a dozen visitors and a guide whose name tag told us he might be related to someone out of our past. The connection proved fascinating, one of those moments that brings an answer to a question you've relegated to the unanswerable. That story is for another time.

Mesa Verde is like that: a time/space warp where the unexpected may just fall into place.

56

Long House Granary, Mesa Verde, Colorado

THIS GRANARY SITS HIGH above Long House ruin. Like so many Ancestral Puebloan structures, it was built to fit into and make best use of the natural rock. I imagine Long House's inhabitants climbing into the granary to store corn and other foodstuffs for winter, retrieving them when needed. When I think of a time when food was harvested, stored and eaten in line with need rather than profit, it evokes a less complicated life.

A more principled one?

57

LeConte Glacier Icebergs, Alaska

WE WERE EXPLORING Alaska's Inside Passage on a small ship whose captain loved getting us close enough to glaciers and waterfalls that we could reach over the deck railing and touch them. Or almost.

Today, when clear signs of global warming—receding glaciers, melting polar ice caps, rising seas, ferocious storms—are being discredited by many who prefer the Bible or obscene profit to taking the necessary precautionary measures, I cannot digest the terrifying statistics. They are like the statistics of war, natural disaster, or endless migration: too overwhelming to process.

I think instead of this photograph I made of delicate blue ice embracing a small pool of turquoise water. When gems like this melt, it will mean the end of the polar bear's habitat, the disintegration of shorelines, the erasure of many major cities and some entire island countries, and the loss of species and resources such as the air we breathe, rendering the earth uninhabitable.

COOL COMPRESSES AND NONBINDING LAW

Now the patient's fever spikes at dawn
as well as late afternoon.
Cool compresses and nonbinding law
do nothing to bring it down.
Glaciers melt, filling valleys with oceans of salt.
The patient must sleep upright.
Her lungs no longer expand
or retract in harmony.
Teeth chattering like insulted bone,
she sweats toxic waste
and fracking's poison,
vomits the bile of mutilated seed.
The fire on her brow swallows wilderness,
great cities and small towns.
Branches crackle like charred veins,
science fiction a pale portrait of her agony.
Preventative medicine was the only way
to avoid this fatal turn.
We're years past that now.
Breathtaking no longer means beautiful.
No morphine, hospice or final ritual, this illness

increases dangerous levels of testosterone.
The patient's fever rises off the charts,
her death a matter of time.
Her preventable disease reaches
every orphaned child, every pristine landscape
buried in ash, hurricane or earthquake
off the Richter scale.
A pandemic of rapes and murders opens
like sores on her once fertile body,
desperate migrations push
through permanently clogged arteries.
The patient's echoing warnings
may be observed or not
by some future species
when oblivious time returns.[1]

---

1. *About Little Charlie Lindbergh and Other Poems* (San Antonio: Wings Press, 2014), 99–100.

58

Caryatids, Acropolis, Athens, Greece

CLIMBING THE HILL TO Athens' Acropolis, we pass people selling local wares, visitors from all over the world, architectural remnants giving us a taste of what's to come. I turn around every now and then to look down upon the agora, where Socrates walked almost two and a half millennia ago, pondering the questions of his time—which remain the questions of mine.

As we enter the area of famous temples, there is a great deal of scaffolding and bracing of buildings in various states of disrepair. So many wonders of the ancient world are in need of attention now. Colonialist superpowers never hesitated to plunder such sites, but the responsibility for keeping them standing falls to each country, countries that often lack the resources needed to protect them.

I want to remember architects and artists, say their names. The Erechtheion Temple was built between 421 and 406 BC by Mnesicles. The sculptor and chief mason was Phidias, who also built the Parthenon. The Erechtheion honored legendary Erechtheus, mentioned in Homer's *Iliad* as a great king and ruler of Athens during the Archaic Period.

This small gem of a temple is built on a slope, such that its west and north sides are about nine feet lower than those on the south and east. This gives it a slightly off-kilter aspect, as if balanced on one foot. It is entirely made of marble from Mount Pentelikon with friezes of black limestone from Eleusis. Every detail is exquisite here, and you marvel even at those places where the stone has weathered or fallen away. Doorways and windows are elaborately carved. Originally, they were also painted: gilded and highlighted with gilt bronze and multicolored glass beads. What we see today is a bleached presentation of what was.

The south porch is what holds my attention. There, six draped female figures—caryatids—are the supporting columns. These caryatids are copies. Five of the originals were taken to the old museum and now reside in the New Acropolis Museum at the foot of the hill, where they can be viewed in climate-controlled conditions on a balcony that allows visitors to contemplate them from all sides. There, sophisticated restoration methods are applied to their surfaces, including the renewal of their decades of rich patina which is achieved with laser technology.

The sixth original figure was removed in 1800 by Britain's Lord Elgin, the same who stole what are known today as the Elgin Marbles, valuable friezes taken from the nearby Parthenon. This sixth figure remains in the British Museum in London. Athenian legend has it that each night the five remaining caryatids can be heard wailing for their lost sister. At the temple, this sixth figure is a visible absence. In my picture, as often happens with the magic of photography, she appears as a dark featureless cutout against the blue sky.

The caryatids, or draped maidens, are individuals, each with her own expression and slightly different details of dress. When I think of the Chinese affirmation that women hold up half the sky, I think of these figures supporting a dome of sky, still a glass ceiling, cracked but unbroken.

59

Blue-Footed Booby
Mother and Chick,
Galápagos Islands, Ecuador

I HAVE CALLED THIS photograph "The Flying Lesson." On the Galápagos Islands, the native birds and animals own their habitat. We must stay on marked paths, move only with the permission of our naturalist guide, respect the space and habits of the wildlife we have come to observe. This duo's repeated gestures were clear: the chick flapped its small wings, then waited for its mother's approval before trying again. The adult bird perched on a stone, giving it the advantage of height as it imparted a teaching that would define its offspring's life.

Like so many such sites, Galápagos National Park is caught between competing interests: tourism's immense contribution to Ecuador's national coffers, the demands of ecologists and others trying to protect the uniqueness of the place, and the fishing industry with its own set of requirements. We were fortunate to visit for the first time almost two decades ago, before the large cruise ships invaded these pristine waters and more than a group or two of visitors were permitted to be on an island at any time.

There are fewer and fewer places on earth today where outsiders can get close to indigenous peoples or animals without the contact destroying the latter's culture and threatening their survival. Isolation can be protective or self-defeating. As the invaders, we so often make decisions that destroy the very reality we've come to see.

60

Giant Tortoise, Galápagos Islands, Ecuador

WE WERE HAVING LUNCH at an open-air eatery in the highlands of the large island of Santa Cruz. Suddenly someone shouted: "The tortoises are nearby! Let's go!" We left half-eaten food on our plates and piled back into our minibus. Within minutes, we were in a large field, among dozens of the great beings moving slowly beneath their weathered shells. They were making their way back down to the sea.

They seemed to ignore us, even when we crouched close. Millennial intuition and purpose. Still, I sensed a communion, a wordless interaction between these ancient reptiles and us. It was as if they breathed out as we breathed in, our very different lungs in some inexplicable relationship. They are plodding, we move quickly, they are patient, while we are eager. Yet something links us, something unknowable, waiting.

61

Marine Iguanas,
Galápagos Islands, Ecuador

SIZE CONFUSES. If these marine iguanas were larger, they might bring dinosaurs to mind. But the largest are only a couple of feet from head to tail. It is their numbers that astound: vistas of hundreds sunning themselves on sun-bleached rocks, often piled upon one another as if community is paramount. Indeed, it must be. These two seem to be a couple: lovers or close friends. Even as I see them in relationship, I am reminded of how foolish it is to ascribe human characteristics to other species.

62

Hiking Shoes and Hat

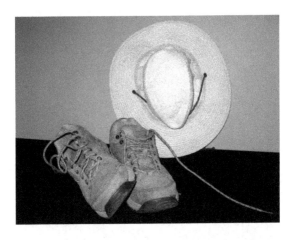

FOR MUCH OF MY LIFE, I avoided physical activity. I'm still not sure why. Maybe because my parents never encouraged it. I was an awkward teenager who dreaded gym class at school because I was invariably picked last when teams were chosen. Standing alone in the gym or on the playground brought a feeling of isolation. I wasn't good at any sport except swimming and archery. I often forged doctor's notes excusing me from participation for one invented reason or another. Cause and effect became a vicious cycle in this area of my life.

As I grew into adulthood, this resistance to physical activity continued. My friends said of me, "Oh sure, Margaret loves to walk: from the front door to the car!" Then, when I was fifty, Barbara came into my life. She loved biking and hiking. I cannot remember her ever urging me to join her, and that's undoubtedly why I did. She was encouraging without being demanding. The first time I managed two blocks on a bicycle, she didn't try to get me to ride two more, but enthusiastically praised what I'd done.

One day, when we'd been together for a couple of years, I said I wanted to lose weight. We started going to a gym at 4:30 each morning, so we could work out and be back home before she had to leave for work. I lost forty or fifty pounds, enough so I felt more comfortable using my body. Hiking quickly became my outdoor activity of choice. For several years I enjoyed biking with Barbara, but hiking was my first love. I had long felt a deep connection with the desert where I live. Now I could explore it on foot, experience it more intimately, discover some of its secrets.

During my hiking years, now behind me, I had several pairs of boots or shoes and several hats. These are the most recent. Sadly, they are relics now.

AT EVERY SWITCHBACK ON THE TRAIL

the journey writes a different poem.
Through every hollow
my silver cord raises its voice
in broken harmony:
new voice, changed song
keeping me coming back
for more.
Ravens who flew with me in March

gone now, without remorse.
An ancient sun
heats my body with fierce intensity.
I take your hand
and the center of my world
shifts imperceptibly.[1]

---

1. *Where They Left You for Dead / Halfway Home,* 101.

63

La Luz Trail, Sandia Mountains, New Mexico

THE TRAILHEAD, JUST EAST of Albuquerque, is at 6,000 feet. The end of the eight-mile trail is at 10,000, a 4,000-foot gain over a dramatically changing landscape that moves from desert scrub through tall pines and then bald-faced rock where vegetation thins again. It took me more than a year to get to Sandia Crest, advancing a bit more each time I attempted it. I got to know La Luz in every season but mid-winter, when hiking the upper region is not permitted due to snow and ice on the portion known as the rockslide: a debris field of loose stone and scree. Luz is Spanish for light. La Luz: the light.

Here it is fall and patches of aspen are in full gold. The feature in the background is called The Thumb and you sometimes see rock climbers on its face. I will always remember one midday picnicking in a clearing across from The Thumb. As I ate my sandwich, I watched two climbers moving gracefully up its wall. That evening's local news brought a report that both had fallen to their deaths. I kept thinking: "But just hours earlier I saw them alive." I couldn't reconcile that brief passage of time between life and death. By the time I stopped hiking, I had climbed La Luz a couple of dozen times. Each was adventure and accomplishment.

I miss those hikes, some made in the company of Barbara or friends, many made alone, where nothing came between me and the land I love.

LIGHT

Light fills me now, spills from my mouth:
wave train
before a rapid.
Crystal darts across this canyon floor
wiping shadow from red rock cleft,
spitting questions.
Desert light sounds Grandmother flute,
her dancing mirror
of blown glass.

Dawn's transparent metal, passionate by noon,
paints sand and stone
leaps through falling water.
Sky full of stars spits silver
through dark foliage
of gamble oak.[1]

1. "Light," in *Stones Witness* (Tucson: University of Arizona Press, 2007), 61.

64

Plitvice Lakes, Croatia

WHEN WE DECIDED TO travel the Adriatic Coast on a small ship that embarked in Greece and made stops in Montenegro, Albania, and Croatia, we expected a tranquil journey. We'd seen pictures of Dubrovnik's walled city and knew we would be enchanted by Zagreb. But we weren't prepared for Albania's surreal countryside or some of the other surprises we encountered.

Plitvice Lakes are a series of turquoise pools, some so clear you can see schools of golden fish deep beneath their surface. Visitors walk endless wooden slatted pathways past one storybook scene after another. Waterfalls cascade through lush vegetation. This photograph is misleading, as so many are, because I focused on the natural beauty and avoided including the solid stream of tourists in my frame.

I was exhausted at the end of the three-hour hike. I was also delighted to have discovered this extraordinary place.

65

Roman Ruin,
Butrint, Albania

ALBANIA, AS I SAY, was surreal. During its time as part of the Soviet Bloc, it had been cut off from the rest of the world. The stories emerging from Enver Hoxha's regime painted him as a beloved leader or ruthless dictator, depending on who was doing the telling. After the implosion of Soviet-style socialism, a good friend traveled through many of the Eastern European capitals trying to understand what life there had been like and what the future might hold for peoples dedicated to creating social justice but in many ways stopped in time.[1] His book

---

1. Stan Persky, *Then We Take Berlin: Stories from the Other Side of Europe* (Toronto: Alfred A. Knopf Canada, 1995).

contains the touching story of two elderly translators who worked for years rendering Hoxha's speeches into English. At night, to keep themselves sane, they translated Shakespeare and other classics.

During our brief time in Albania, we traveled a highway that often resembled an unpaved country road. Someone in our group was startled when he tried to determine our location using his cellphone's GPS. "We are nowhere," he announced, genuinely perplexed. Rusted out bomb shelters bordered this highway. It was rumored that Hoxha, in his paranoia, had used all the cement in the country to build the refuges. Each had been large enough to shelter a couple of people at most. Occasionally we passed large half-finished homes, upended by bulldozers and abandoned at awkward angles. Our guide told us these building projects had been interrupted when one level of corruption collided with another. "But if I had to choose between a Communist-era apartment and one built today," she added, "I would take the one constructed under Hoxha anytime. I know it would be built responsibly, of better materials, more solid and lasting."

We were headed for the Roman ruins at Butrint. Mysterious and evocative as all ruins are, they projected a time long before socialism and capitalism fought on the world stage and capitalism won. We spent several hours walking through those ruins, admiring the ancient architecture with its graceful arches. I was surprised by an elderly woman sitting behind a rickety card table at the entrance to the site. Seeming utterly out of place, she was selling cheap pieces of jewelry fashioned from silver filigree.

"Authentic communist jewelry," she repeated in English as each of us straggled by. I wondered if she considered Albania's socialist era to be prehistory or a time she remembered with nostalgia.

66

EZLN Virgin of Guadalupe, Chiapas, Mexico

THE VIRGIN OF GUADALUPE, also called Our Lady of Guadalupe, is the patron saint of Mexico and is popular throughout Latin America and in Latinx neighborhoods in the United States. The story is that a poor Indian widower named Cuauhtlatohuac was baptized into the Catholic faith and given the name of Juan Diego. On the morning of December 9th, 1531, he was walking to a nearby church to attend a mass in honor of Our Lady. As he walked up Tepeyac Hill he heard beautiful music, like a chorus of singing birds. A luminous cloud appeared and within it stood an Indian maiden dressed like an Aztec princess. The maiden spoke to him in his native tongue and told him to seek an audience with the bishop of Mexico, a Franciscan named Juan de Zumarraga. Juan Diego was to tell him to build a chapel in the place where the maiden appeared.

Bishop de Zumarraga demanded a sign. The Virgin appeared once more to Juan Diego and gave him a bouquet of roses to carry in his cape or *tilma* to the bishop. On December 12th, when Juan Diego opened his cape in the bishop's presence, the roses fell to the ground and the bishop, recognizing them as the sign he had asked for, fell to his knees. On Juan Diego's *tilma*, an image of Mary appeared exactly as she had appeared to him on Tepeyac Hill.

In the Virgin of Guadalupe, Mexicans see proof that Mary belongs to all peoples, the poor as well as the wealthy who, before she appeared, venerated more Europeanized virgins brought from Spain. In the context of Spanish colonialism, the Virgin of Guadalupe functioned as a rebuke to colonialism's cruelty. An immense church was built at Tepeyac, where the popular Virgin appeared to Juan Diego. Each year on December 12th, thousands of people make their way to the shrine, many of them on their knees.

Many artists, innovative as well as traditional, have depicted the Virgin of Guadalupe in paintings and prints. Chicana Alma López painted her in a bikini, causing a public tug of war between the Santa Fe New Mexico Museum displaying the piece and that city's Catholic hierarchy that demanded it be removed. Likenesses of the Virgin of Guadalupe can be found in tattoos, on candles, and many other objects. These may vary according to the cultures of their creators, but rarely reach the level of identification or supposed disrespect embodied in López's rendition.

On January 1st, 1994, members of the Zapatista Army of National Liberation (EZLN, in its Spanish acronym) attacked government installations and tried to free political prisoners in the town of San Cristobal de las Casas, Chiapas, southern Mexico. The movement had been organized a decade earlier by a number of Lacandón Indians and a mysterious figure who referred to himself as Subcomandante Marcos. The EZLN came to national prominence in response to the establishment of NAFTA (the North American Free Trade Alliance) that, it said, was unfair to Mexican workers.

The EZLN sought autonomy for indigenous peoples all over Mexico but wasn't your typical liberation organization. It fought neither for state power nor for victory over the national government but was defensive in its efforts to make a better life for the people of the region. Rather than follow a Marxist ideology, it retrieved ancient forms of community organizing. Over the next decade or so, the EZLN created schools, clinics, and workers cooperatives. Women were prominent in the movement and it was said they enjoyed equal rights with men. Support came from all over the world. Many well-known intellectuals and artists went to Chiapas to see for themselves what the Zapatistas were about. In time, Marcos retired from the Zapatista leadership. The movement continues. It's still not clear exactly who he was.

As with the syncretism between indigenous and Christian practices throughout the world, there has been a syncretism between deeply-rooted cultural symbols and revolutionary movements. This small painted image of the Virgin of Guadalupe, her face covered by a revolutionary handkerchief, is one such example. It was given to me by a friend who spent time with the Zapatistas in the Lacandón jungle and sold their creations to the outside world to help them raise funds.

67

Masks, León, Nicaragua

THE TWO CHILDREN WEARING masks are so prominent in this photograph you don't immediately notice that
four faces are not wearing them. One boy is effectively
stretching his own features into a mask-like semblance. It's
1983 and carnival time in León, Nicaragua. I've lived in
the country for more than two years by the time I make this
image and am beginning to have a feel for its cultural idiosyncrasies. On holidays, you can always sense an intense
urge to celebrate, as much on the part of those who have
the appropriate attire as on the part of those who don't.

After the Cuban Revolution, democratic elections in Chile strengthened the socialist presence in Latin America. But Chile's success was short-lived. Only three years after Salvador Allende entered La Moneda—the seat of Chilean government—he was imprisoned there with no alternative but to take his own life. His final speech to the nation, in which he promised that "one day the great avenues will part, and the people will march through," still sounded in our devastated ears. And then, a few years later in 1979—all this continental-wide struggle took place in the 1970s—we had Nicaragua. The Sandinistas were victorious in July of that year, extending once again our hope for continental change.

I was close to the Sandinistas in Cuba prior to their win, and very curious about what their revolution would look like. It was now twenty years after the Cuban Revolution had come to power. In Nicaragua, many more women had taken up arms, and feminism wasn't a dirty word. An important Christian presence was palpable, linked to struggle by Vatican II, and it imbued Sandinista policies with a humanism not present in the early years of the Cuban Revolution. The country also had a vibrant indigenous population, particularly on its Atlantic coast while the native Cubans had been eradicated early on. My old friend, Ernesto Cardenal, was the country's first Minister of Culture. He was also one of the greatest living poets of the language. And, only a couple of months after the end of the war, he had invited me to come talk to his country's women, listen to their stories of participation, write about them.[1]

---

1. Still living in Cuba, I had written *Inside the Nicaraguan Revolution: The Story of Doris Tijerino* (1978). After my 1979 fieldwork in

I had many reasons for wanting to experience what was happening in Nicaragua. I brought my youngest daughter, Ana, with me when I moved there at the end of 1980. My daughter Ximena joined us the following year. I also brought my newly acquired photographer's skills. I had only apprenticed to the Cuban photographer who had been my mentor for a few short months when I began shooting pictures of Sandinistas in many walks of life. They had all sorts of ideas about how to remake their country. But I continued to learn on the ground. Most of my iconic images reflect the intensity of those first years of revolution in Nicaragua. This remains one of my favorites.

Nicaragua, I produced *Sandino's Daughters* (1981), my most popular title to date and published in a number of languages. In subsequent years I came out with *Christians in the Nicaraguan Revolution* (1983), *Risking a Somersault in the Air: Conversations with Nicaraguan Writers* (1984), and *Sandino's Daughters Revisited* (1994). Ernesto Cardenal died on March 1st, 2020.

68

Sandinista Certificate, Nicaragua

IF THE PRECEDING OBJECT, my photograph of children, speaks to me of creativity and hope, this certificate is important to me for precisely the opposite reason. I was proud of it at the time, but in retrospect it seems prophetic of doom. In 1989, I no longer lived in Nicaragua, having returned to the United States five years earlier. But on the Sandinista Revolution's 10th anniversary, it gave certificates like this one to those of us who had lent our support and participation to that great revolutionary effort. I received mine back home, just a few months before winning the battle to regain my US citizenship.

The certificate is bittersweet. It brings to mind genuine Sandinistas who were close friends and died before they could see victory. It evokes memories of honest struggle by so many and makes me think of the legitimate Sandinistas who today work in isolation in a country ruled by tyrants. By 1989, the revolutionary spirit we knew and loved had succumbed to outside pressures and its own internal problems. By the following year, it was voted out of office. And since then, despite realignments of various sorts, it has never managed to recreate itself in anything but a skewed version of its former self.

Today, Nicaraguans struggle against an authoritarian regime that calls itself Sandinista but is proving to be as cruel a dictatorship as Somoza's. Daniel Ortega and Rosario Murillo—Ortega's wife and vice president—will do anything to remain in power. They have unleashed paramilitary violence on the civilian population, killing and maiming. They have attacked many independent institutions and media outlets, taken hundreds of political prisoners, and forced hundreds more to leave the country. People continue to protest or oppose the regime but, as in the case of Venezuela, much of the US left and much of the Latin American left continue to support an administration that is progressive in name only. And the US government, as always, continues its destabilization efforts. It will do anything and everything to bring these nations back into its sphere of influence.

Sadly, we who fight for justice have yet to develop a model capable of withstanding imperialist pressure and internal erosion. This certificate is a palpable reminder of that tragic reality.

69

Tiny Turquoise Bear Fetish

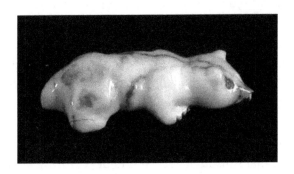

OWL AND HUMMINGBIRD. Duck. Quail. Bald Eagle. Bison or buffalo, especially the rare white buffalo. Frog. Mountain Sheep. Coyote, howling or not. Mole god. And bear, lots of bear. The Zuni people are famous for carving fetishes from turquoise, jet, and other stones. The Hopi and some of the other pueblos also produce these small talismans or amulets. Something between a good luck charm and recognition of a person's animal avatar. Many fetishes sport medicine bundles, bits of feather and stone tied around their midsections as added protection. A thriving fetish tourist trade blurs the line between how Native Americans use these figures and what they mean to the uninitiated.

My fetish is a tiny turquoise bear. I've had it for many years. It doesn't stand tall like most bear fetishes, nor does it carry a medicine bundle. It looks purposefully out of its infinitesimal black dot eyes as it slinks along the ground as if searching a route forward. Its body is laced with matrix, dark veins that some take for imperfection but those familiar with turquoise know add value — or at least interest — to the stone. Over the years, I have pushed this tiny bear deep down into my Levi's pocket when going to a job interview or waiting for a response from a publisher or the results of a biopsy. I do not believe it influences outcomes, only that it comforts me. It has accompanied me in moments of risk and desire, keeping me connected to my most optimistic self.

70

"American Girl in Italy" by Ruth Orkin, 1951

THIS ICONIC PHOTOGRAPH became an object in my life when I glued a postcard-sized copy to a piece of plywood and propped it on my writing desk.

I have read the story of how this photograph was made from the viewpoint of the woman in it. Ninalee Craig met Ruth Orkin in Florence in 1951. There weren't many American women in that city at the time; the two of them were exceptions. They happened to coincide at the American Express office, a place where tourists picked up mail and cashed travelers' checks in those pre-money-machine-and-credit-card days. They started talking and realized they were staying at the same hotel, a place that charged one dollar a day including food. Conversing, Orkin wondered if Craig would be willing to model for her by simply walking along a stretch of city sidewalk. "You know what," Craig remembers Orkin saying, "I bet I could make some money if we just horse around and show what it's like to be a woman alone." Craig was glad to oblige. Decades later, she maintains it was an adventure. When people ask if she was afraid, she always says no.

Craig clutched at her shawl and leather shoulder bag as she moved, head held high, eyes straight ahead, through a phalanx of men leering at her from every direction. I count thirteen of them in various states of aggressive posture. They are standing in doorways or at the curb, seated at a sidewalk cafe table, mounted on a parked motor scooter. You can almost hear the catcalls and whistles.

Orkin is said to have obtained her image on the first or second try. It ran in a 1952 *Cosmopolitan Magazine* photo essay headlined "When You Travel Alone," that offered tips on "money, men and morals to see you through a gay trip and a safe one." The photo caption reflects the cultural mores of the era: "Public admiration [...] shouldn't fluster you. Ogling the ladies is a popular, harmless and flattering pastime you'll run into in many foreign countries. The gentlemen are usually louder and more demonstrative than American men, but they mean no harm."

Two American women, one in front of and the other behind the camera, collaborated on an adventure they both considered good fun. Later, back in the States, they reconnected and remained friends until Orkin's death in 1985. It would be more than half a century before women linked the possessive male gestures that we see in this photo with the misogyny they reflect; the very real and ever-present danger male entitlement encourages, the centuries of coverup that has meant submission and sexual slavery for women throughout the world. Now we have #MeToo. But in many countries, women are still sold into marriage, stoned to death for adultery, denied the freedom to go out alone or to drive. Here in the US, women still get harassed, battered, and raped in shocking numbers. Women still earn less for the same work and are denied employment when pregnant.

"American Girl in Italy" reminds me it remains a man's world, even as women rise.

71

Barbara's Art

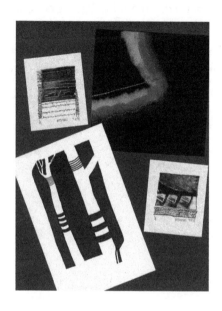

LOVING AN ARTIST IS an extraordinary experience. Living with an artist means every day holds fresh discovery. Neither Barbara nor I were able to dedicate ourselves fulltime to our art until after we retired. I taught at a series of US universities until 1994. She taught public middle school special education students for twenty years. Then each of us made the transition to doing what we were born to do. Now we spend most of our days in side-by-side studios, coming together for meals and to look at one another's work. Our trust has made us one another's best critics.

This selection of four of Barbara's drawings is entirely arbitrary. I could have easily chosen a different four. These are not objects in the conventional sense, but rather representative of what she has been doing of late. A long series of trees. A new medium on the iPad. Asemic writing overlaid on one-of-a-kind Gelli prints.

Living with an artist is like living beside a rushing river that constantly brings new wonders to its surface.

72

My Levi's

THEY HAVE BECOME my daily dress, an object I wear on my body. Comfort, simplicity, and a wide temperature range make them ideal in any season. When one of my two pair needs washing, I switch it out for the other. Only on very rare and very formal occasions do I wear a different style of pants. Levi's fit well with my rejection of the profit-motivated fashion industry. They allow me to be myself.

73

Turquoise Earrings

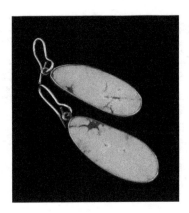

YEARS AGO, I WORE simple turquoise slabs sold by New Mexico's indigenous people on the streets of Albuquerque and Santa Fe. I usually preferred the blue turquoise to the green, liked the mysterious veins of brown matrix running through the stone. When I came home in 1984, a pair that was just the right color and shape could be had for $11. I kept several around in case I lost one.

Gradually, prices rose and the quality of the stones became less desirable. Eventually, I had to buy this pair of thin slabs with silver backs in order to get the size and shape that suited me. These earrings, like my Levi's, are part of my everyday uniform. I have bought many earrings over the years and have been given just as many. I love them all but rarely wear any but these.

74

Apple Laptop

THESE DAYS I WRITE on a large Apple desktop. Its big screen allows me to translate with texts open beside each other and to work in Photoshop with ease. This is the laptop with which I travel. I don't overload it with all my programs or files, just what I'm working on at the moment. More than simply an object, it's my lifeline to the world: my email connection with children, grandchildren, greatgrandchildren, friends, publishers, and what passes for news. I used to have a smaller version with an 11-inch monitor. But part of Apple's business model is built-in obsolescence, so we always have to buy a newer version. When Apple stopped making that ideal model that weighed less than a pound, the smallest available replacement was this. It has a 13-inch monitor and is quite a bit heavier.

I often get irritated with myself at having become dependent on Apple's ruthless business model, but I appreciate what computers have done for my writing. It's been a long journey since that 1940's Royal portable typewriter.

75

El Corno Emplumado #26

WHEN I REMEMBER *El Corno Emplumado,* the bi-lingual literary journal I co-founded and co-edited out of Mexico City in the 1960s, I remember thirty-one separate objects. We managed to produce thirty-one quarterly issues, almost all with between two and three hundred pages. We published more than seven hundred writers from more than thirty countries, some extremely well-known, others complete newcomers—some of whom would become luminaries in their lifetimes. The journal was part of a cultural renaissance that exploded throughout the world in those years. My co-founder and co-editor,

Sergio Mondragón, and I were twenty-six and twenty-five years old when we embarked on the impossible mission. Today, fifty years after the journal's demise, poets and readers in many places still celebrate its impact and reach.

This is the cover of issue #26. We took the image from an iconic poster designed by Alfredo Rostgaard for Cuba's New Song Movement. The rose with the drop of blood falling from a thorn says it all. We felt free in those days to use images we loved without asking permission from anyone. *El Corno Emplumado* spoke for several generations. Many continue to hear its voice.[1]

---

1. Go to https://opendoor.northwestern.edu/archive/ to see the complete run of the journal in facsimile.

76

Mudhead Kachina Doll, Hopi, Arizona

KACHINA OR KATSINA DOLLS were traditionally carved from lightweight cottonwood root and represented the spirits of each figure in Hopi, Zuni, or other tribal dances and ceremonies. The older figures, referred to as Early Traditional Style, date back to the late 19th and early 20th centuries. They were the most usual depiction of the katsinam before outsiders brought their influences to bear on the Native American cultures. Those early dolls were flatter, with fewer three-dimensional elements. A head often topped a formless body. The dyes and pigments used in painting them came from native minerals like iron, magnesium, and plant-based substances. The New Traditional Style, of which this Mudhead is an example, is rooted in the old ways, although the dolls have more detail and the artists use synthetic paints and modern painting techniques.

The Koyemsi, or Mudhead, is a clown seen in most Hopi ceremonies. It drums, dances, and plays games with the audience. Its presence is humorous, and it often tells jokes or off-color stories. The Mudhead is "the people's spirit." Mudheads often form a chorus of accompaniment. If a dancer arrives late or doesn't have the proper mask, he can easily become a Mudhead by donning that figure's headpiece, resembling a clay sphere of mud.

I bought this kachina years ago at the Hubbell Trading Post at Ganado, Arizona. I saw it there, thought about it for a while, left, then turned around twenty miles down the road, knowing I must return to claim what belonged to me.

77

Book Bag from City Lights, San Francisco, California

CITY LIGHTS IS EXEMPLARY among progressive independent literary bookstores in the United States. Its history is intimately linked to half a century of waves of new writing in the country, particularly that of the Beat generation. Still at its original address on Columbus Avenue in San Francisco, it was founded in 1953 by Lawrence Ferlinghetti and Peter Martin. It was declared a National Heritage site in 2001.

The store gained nationwide notoriety or fame for publishing Allen Ginsberg's *Howl* in its Pocket Poets Series in 1956. In 1957, local Collector of Customs Chester MacPhee seized a shipment of the book's second printing from England on the grounds of obscenity. He was made to release the shipment when federal authorities refused to confirm his charge. But in June of that year, local police raided City Lights and arrested store manager Shigeyoshi Murao on charges of selling an obscene book. Murao was later freed because it couldn't be proven that he knew what was in it.

Ferlinghetti, as publisher, didn't get off so easily. When he heard that his store manager had been arrested, he turned himself in. His trial ran from August 16th to September 3rd, 1957. Many respected writers and professors testified in his defense. Judge Horn delivered a precedent-setting verdict, declaring that *Howl* was not obscene and that any book with "the slightest redeeming social importance" deserves First Amendment protection. The decision was important for many books of that era, when writers were defying the strictures placed on them by McCarthyism and other aspects of suffocating postwar morality. *Howl* has been translated into twenty-four languages and has sold more than a million copies to date.

City Lights has an unparalleled stock and indescribable atmosphere. You can spend hours browsing its several rooms. I have read there twice, first in 2013 when I presented *The Rhizome as a Field of Broken Bones* and again in 2018 when I launched *Time's Language: Selected Poems 1959–2018*. Both were exuberant experiences. Reading surrounded by shelves holding one of the world's most complete collections of poetry books and magazines, I felt a tremendous creative energy. It was as if I was breathing in the voices of poets from every language and tradition.

Every time I use this book bag, I feel poetry's magic running through my veins.

78

Medal for Literary Merit, Chihuahua, Mexico

EACH YEAR, THE LITERATURA en el Bravo festival awards its Medal for Literary Merit to a poet it deems worthy of the large silver disk. Curiously, the letter I received telling me I'd been chosen mentioned the exact amount of silver it would contain. Past winners have included Juan Gelman, Jerome Rothenberg, and Amparo Dávila. I was given the medal in 2017. I was stunned and deeply honored. Two of my daughters, Ximena and Sarah, flew to Ciudad Juárez to accompany me. Several dear friends came as well, including María Vázquez Valdez from Mexico City, Víctor Rodríguez Núñez and Kate Hedeen from Ohio, Joe Richey and Anne Becher who traveled by bus from Boulder, Colorado, and Mike Moye who drove down from Albuquerque. My wife Barbara was at my side.

I remember thinking about what I would say in my brief words of acceptance. In recent years, Ciudad Juárez, where the festival takes place, had been plagued with hundreds of unsolved murders of young women. I wanted to honor their memories yet felt it might not be appropriate for me—an outsider—to bring up the painful subject. I was relieved, then, when the representative of the governor of the state of Chihuahua, who had placed the medal around my neck, did so. She remembered an old book of mine, *Las mujeres*, and talked about how that introduction to feminism helped generations of Mexican women become strong in their understanding of gender and resistance to violence.[1]

I have received very few literary distinctions in the United States, many more in Latin America.

---

1. *Las mujeres* (Mexico City: Siglo XXI Editores SA, 1970).

79

Time's Language: Selected Poems (1959–2018)

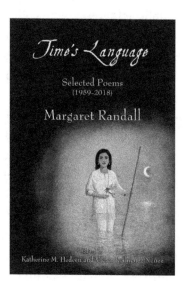

I'VE KNOWN Víctor Rodríguez Núñez since he was seventeen years old and he and other young poets spent most evenings at my Havana apartment. We were a close-knit group, reading to one another, critiquing each other's work, eventually starting a Saturday writing workshop on the grounds of the University of Havana. Víctor remembers that I gave him his first typewriter. It must have been the old Olympia portable I had at the time. We've stayed in touch over the years. Today he is one of Cuba's most important poetic voices. When he married Kathrine M.

Hedeen, they made the perfect literary couple, collaborating on translating poetry in both directions.

I can't remember when Víctor and Kate first suggested that it might be interesting to assemble selections from my poetry books to date. I said go ahead, and they did. But no publisher was interested. Five or six years later, one was. By then I had published several more collections. Víctor and Kate revised what they already had and added new work. From then on, many loving hands collaborated to make *Time's Language* the beautiful volume it is. You can travel sixty years of my journey in poetry, through 450 pages hardbound in a book that also contains an introduction, chronology, and a dozen photographs. Several friends contributed money to allow the book to be sold at an accessible price. My wife Barbara lent one of her beautiful motifs to the cover. Bryce Milligan of Wings Press designed every page with his customary artistry and care.

Thumbing through *Time's Language: Selected Poems 1959–2018*, I cringe at my incipient early poems and happily trace my journey to a more mature voice in recent work. I launched the book at City Lights in San Francisco, Bluestockings in New York, Collected Works in Santa Fe, and Bookworks in Albuquerque. I'm grateful to Víctor, Kate, Bryce, and others who in one way or another curated this journey.

80

Only the Road / Solo el camino: Eight Decades of Cuban Poetry

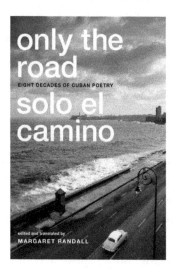

AS MUST BE EVIDENT by now, books are also objects to me—beautiful objects with which I enjoy curling up at the corner of my couch to finger their pages, smell their ink, and admire their design as well as devour their contents.

I started translating Spanish poetry into English years ago, when Sergio and I edited El Corno Emplumado. We often worked together and loved being able to offer exciting new work written in one language in translation in the other. After moving to Cuba, I continued to translate, producing two anthologies of Cuban poetry in English. Then came many years in which I read the translations of others but rarely ventured into that field myself. In 2014, Duke University Press asked me to translate a memoir by a Peruvian anthropologist, and a novel by a writer from the Dominican Republic a couple of years later. Not long after, I was moved to render the work of several Cuban poets in bilingual editions. These books followed one another in rapid succession. I love Cuban poetry and wondered if I could tackle a definitive anthology. I wondered even more if a publisher would be willing to take such an anthology on.

When my editor at Duke showed interest, I began working in earnest. *Only the Road / Solo el camino* showcases eight decades of Cuban poets in five hundred pages. My aim was to present enough poems by each so that readers will have a feel for their work. My two oldest poets were born in 1902, the youngest in 1981. Poets from every region of the country, several races and ethnic backgrounds, and a range of gender identities speak here, and close to half of the fifty-six poets included are women.

This book/object represents the many books I have translated from Spanish into English.

81

I Never Left Home:
Poet, Feminist, Revolutionary

I DIDN'T START OUT writing a memoir. A friend suggested I write about my time among the abstract expressionists in New York City. Believing the Sixties (by which I mean the period beginning in the late '50s and ending mid-1970s) have been misrepresented by most of those who have written about them, it was something I'd long wanted to do. I began by writing what I thought was a personal essay about that time. Barbara knew I was writing a memoir; I didn't.

When I'd done all that I felt I could with my time in New York, I found myself moving on to my years in Mexico. By this time, I suspected Barbara was right. And

I continued with my decade in Cuba. Chronologically, Nicaragua should have come next. But that's where I hit a wall. Residual PTSD from the Contra war that was gripping the country just before I left made it difficult to remember details, bring images into sharp focus. So I went back to my childhood and adolescence. I realized I wanted to write about what life was like for girls and women in 1950s America, that stifling weight of misogyny.

I was writing a memoir, shaping and nurturing it, choosing what I wanted to include and what to leave out. At a certain point I told a longtime friend, now living in Spoleto, about my project. "But I have a memoir you sent me twenty years ago," he responded, "you must have a copy too. It's 607 pages long!" I neither had a copy nor could I remember having written such a book. He said he would send it to me. "No," I said, "I don't trust the mails." And so my friend bought a scanner and scanned every one of those 607 pages, sending me jpegs in groups of forty or fifty. I placed them all in a three-ring binder and read that twenty-year-old manuscript. I recognized the writing and the person doing the writing. But I still couldn't remember having produced it.

I was glad that older book had never found a publisher. I couldn't identify with its voice or tone. I was no longer interested in writing only about myself but wanted to produce a book in which time and place are as much protagonists as the author.

I Never Left Home is the result.

82

Margaret's and Barbara's Wedding Bands

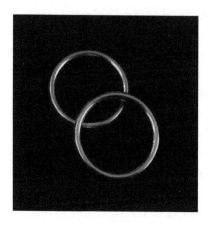

JUST WEEKS AFTER WE got together in 1986, Barbara and I confessed to one another that we wanted rings. Mary Elizabeth Jane Colter came to me in a dream. She said we'd find our rings at Grand Canyon. We drove over, seven and a half hours in January cold. And we did find the first rings we wore. They were waiting for us—just two, and in our respective sizes—at a beautiful shop on the south rim called Hopi House and built by the beloved architect. Those rings were simple silver bands with bear prints circling them in Hopi overlay. They cost thirty dollars each. We loved them but the silver was so soft that they fell apart after a few years.

We replaced those first rings with others: sturdier silver overlay designed by a contemporary artist, followed by slender bands of lapis lazuli and finally others of silver with a thin gold wash across half the band. We shared the latter with our friend Jane Norling, who bought a matching one for herself. Then, a few years back, one US state after another began embracing marriage equality. The federal government finally caught up, and lesbian and gay male couples, many of whom had been living together for decades, were able to marry. Barbara and I decided to do so at my daughter Ana's home in Brooklyn. In the presence of family and friends, we legalized a relationship already twenty-eight years old.

Another opportunity to buy rings, this time for the duration. I'm not sure why we chose these simple gold bands, as conventional and ordinary as wedding rings can be. Neither one of us has been able to fully grasp why the ceremony was so important to us either; we certainly don't favor state sanction over our own. Or why our rings are the talisman closest to each of our hearts. Sometimes I find myself nudging mine with the thumb of my left hand. The gesture provides immense comfort.

83

Rano Raraku, Rapa Nui

IN 2007, STILL READING the paper edition of the *New York Times*, I opened its travel section and saw a piece by playwright Edward Albee. He was writing about a recent trip he'd made to Rapa Nui and described it as having been life changing. Rapa Nui, known more popularly as Easter Island, is a tiny dot of land in the south-central Pacific. The single small town, Hanga Roa, is home to some 5,000 inhabitants. They share their ten by fifteen square-mile island with hundreds of immense stone monoliths, the famous moais that dot the countryside or line up sentinel-like along the coastline, facing inland against a backdrop of vast ocean.

I immediately knew I had to visit Rapa Nui. Traveling to the island isn't easy. You can fly south to Santiago, Chile, and then west to the airstrip at Hang Roa, or west to Tahiti and then on to the remote island. Rapa Nui is owned by Chile and depends on that South American nation for shipments of foodstuff and other necessities. More than a decade ago when we visited, it was yet to become a major tourist destination. I was astonished, upon our arrival, to discover that Rapa Nui is in the same time zone as Albuquerque.

Not everything is known—or remembered—about Rapa Nui. In 1200 AD, an adventurous group of Polynesians arrived on raft-like boats with nothing but the night sky to guide them. Others say earlier, around 800. There were trees on the island then, but settlers eventually cut them all down to make their seafaring vessels. Recent social anthropologists blame them for having done this. They make them responsible for their own demise. I ask: what choice did they have?

In more modern times, the incursions of explorers are well documented. In 1722, a Dutch admiral may have been the first European to encounter the island; he came upon it on Easter Day, thus the name Easter Island. Later English, French, Germans, Russians, Chileans, and North Americans all made claims. In 1862, Peruvians kidnapped 1,500 of Rapa Nui's healthiest men, bringing them to the mainland as slave labor. When protest forced them to return a single starving boatload, the dozen survivors brought smallpox and tuberculosis with them, reducing the population even more.

Our week on Rapa Nui was full of surprises. We'd made reservations at a small family-owned hotel. The owner responded to our need of a four-wheel drive vehicle by telling us his cousin would be glad to rent us one for the week. In that vehicle, we traveled every one of the island's few roads, most of them dirt, and explored every cluster of moais, the quarries from which they'd been cut, and Rapa Nui's two mysterious craters. We climbed into Rano Raraku and realized we were picnicking on the sunken nose of a large moai still half carved and long settled in earth. We hiked to caves where strange figures painted on the walls seemed to dance before our eyes.

At a place called Orongo, we visited berm structures called birdman houses on a high cliff that forms the very lip of Rano Kao overlooking the sea one thousand feet below. We tried to imagine taking part in the yearly birdman ritual in which young men swam out to a spit of rock where a rookery of Manu Tara or Sooty Tern still exists. The men's goal was to retrieve eggs from their nests and swim to shore without breaking them. We talked to locals about what it was like to live so far away from the closest civilization, what they remembered of the old ways, the traditions that were being lost.

I came home and found myself writing poems about Rapa Nui. *Their Backs to the Sea* came out a couple of years later.[1]

---

1. *Their Backs to the Sea* (San Antonio: Wings Press, 2009).

84

Tongariki, Rapa Nui

AT TONGARIKI, YOU GET a sense of how the moais guarded the island at the height of their people's cultural expression. They are lined up in almost regimental fashion atop the ahu, or stone platform, built to support them. One figure still wears the round head piece or top knot called pukao, typical of earlier times. The pukao, which once adorned the heads of most moais, were carved from a rust-red volcanic scoria quarried at a single source: Puna Pao.

> [...] Little grew in that shallow soil: sweet potatoes,
> yams, taro, guava, sugar, and plantains
> in lava-tube caves.
> Chicken and vegetables. Fish and seabirds.

Sailing vessels brought Polynesia, then Norwegian rats
—the shameful delicacy. And much later
sheep: tens of thousands, but not for you.
As if leeching life from rock was not enough
to set family upon family, call forth
survival wars, a taste for human flesh
and successive battles, other arrivals
brought animals not for your sustenance,
languages not for your lips, new rules
that pinned you to careening history.[1]

---

1. Part IV from "Island without a Name," in *Their Backs to the Sea* (San Antonio: Wings Press, 2009), 6.

85

Rongorongo Board, Rapa Nui (replica)

I KNEW THERE WAS no record of a written language, only picture-like symbols carved with shark bone on both sides of small boards called kohau rongorongo. Originals can be seen in museums around the world and in the single small museum on the island. Cheap copies were among the artifacts offered in shops catering to tourists. I wanted to own a copy, but not one of those crude examples. Someone who had been studying Rapa Nui culture for years managed to get me one that more closely resembles the real thing. No one any longer knows what the symbols mean, although some experts believe they describe clan boundaries or have something to do with genealogy. It is the very mystery of the small wooden board that intrigues me.

86

Cork Signing Pen

BARBARA BOUGHT ME this rollerball pen early in our relationship. It is a Tornado by Retro. Stainless steel tips the top and bottom, and the pen itself has no cap but swivels in and out. The soft cork shaft feels warm in my hand. I use it to sign books after poetry readings. It makes me think of the many perfect gifts Barbara has given me over the decades we've been together.

87

My Treadmill

BARBARA LOVES GOING to the gym, where she can visit with people she's seen there for years. Much more of a hermit when it comes to activities such as exercising, I've always preferred to work out at home. I've had this workhorse of a treadmill for years. No fancy gadgets that measure heartrate or blood oxygen, no magazine or book rack that allows you to read while walking. Only the basics.

Age changes us, but we can also regain some former abilities. Although arthritis took possession of my knees and slowed me down for a while, I am happily using my treadmill again, managing more than two miles every day.

88

Lioness,
Hwange, Zimbabwe

WE WATCHED IN SILENCE for almost an hour. The lioness was stalking a zebra, but not for food. Rather, she was teaching her two adolescent cubs to hunt. They mimicked her, slinking silently through tall grass. When they were all close enough to grab the unsuspecting zebra, she turned and led her cubs away. No need to kill when hunger didn't compel it.

A lesson for our species.

89

Honorary Doctorate in Letters, University of New Mexico

I ENTERED THE University of New Mexico fresh out of high school in 1954. It was a dark period in our country. Fear invaded minds and hearts. Senator Joseph McCarthy had launched his ruthless anticommunist purge, costing thousands their careers, their freedom, and in some cases, their lives. Our world of thought, imagination, and intellectual pursuit suffered greatly, and the chill of that era would plague us for years. It still bears responsibility for our inability to respect dissent. University campuses were no exception to that period of intellectual mediocrity. After a couple of semesters, I'd found nothing that could keep me in school. I quit and began a different sort of life: searching out mentors, knowledge, and experience beyond the confines of academia.

Three decades later, having lived and worked in several other countries, I returned to the city of my youth. I still had no degree. But I'd experienced a lot in a number of places where profound social change had taken place and other cultures had embraced me. I'd participated at the cutting edge of artistic and social change, written some fifty books, and thought I had something to offer young people coming up. Not everyone agreed. Although I would teach at such prestigious universities as Trinity College in Hartford, Connecticut, the University of New Mexico only offered me a few adjunct courses. Teaching at Trinity meant I had to leave home almost half of every year and travel a couple of thousand miles to earn a living. Those were hard times for Barbara and me. My homecoming was also complicated by a deportation order issued by the US government, alleging that my writings went "beyond the good order and happiness of the United States," and the ensuing battle to regain citizenship. Five years later, with the support of many, I won my case. But those holding political power in New Mexico at the time feared dissent and were dismissive of my work. They did their best to limit my opportunities.

Time passed. I retired from teaching in 1994 and devoted myself more fully to my writing. In 2017 a UNM professor decided I deserved an honorary doctorate. She rallied likeminded professionals, collected strong letters of recommendation, and put together a compelling case for my receiving the degree. At the time, however, the state was in the hands of an ultra-rightest administration. In 2018, the board of university regents, chosen by a Republican governor, preferred not to give a single honorary degree rather than give one to me. That year, perhaps for the only time in the institution's history, there were no honorary doctorates at the University of New Mexico.

But then everything changed. The 2018 midterm elections put brilliant and energetic humanist Michelle Lujan Grisham in the governor's office. She immediately removed the most egregious regents, replacing them with men and women of stature and humanity. Coincidentally, the University of New Mexico hired Garnett Stokes, the first female president in its 130-year history, also someone of intelligence and drive who was determined to remedy the corruption and wrongs that had held the institution prisoner throughout the preceding years. In spring 2019, I received a letter from President Stokes telling me the university was offering me an honorary doctorate in letters, the highest degree the university bestows.

Commencement on May 11th, 2019, was more emotional than I anticipated. My hometown school, where I'd studied only briefly so many years before and where I hadn't been able to get a teaching job when I needed one, was acknowledging my art, my politics, and my contribution to the community, state, and larger world. Graduating members of the class of 2019 wore indigenous moccasins and silver and turquoise finery, La Raza stoles and Hawaiian leis, proud afros and elegant cornrows. Diversity was palpable. After a brief biography of a life the school had once vilified was read aloud to an arena hold-ing 15,000 people, President Stokes hooded me and placed the diploma in my hands. In Uruguay, Mexico, France, and New York, my children and grandchildren tuned in to a live stream of the ceremony. I only wished my parents had lived to witness the moment.

90

San Rock Art, KwaZulu-Natal, Drakensberg Mountains, South Africa

MULTIPLE OBJECTS OR subjects claim my memory when I look at this image of San painting on a rock wall at a site in the foothills of the Drakensberg Mountains. Perspective and shading seem unusual for images this old.

We traveled to South Africa with our dear friend Mark Behr, so my first thoughts are of him, only a few years later dead of a sudden heart attack much before his time.[1] From a poor family, Mark had spied on the African National

---

1. Mark Behr, 1963–2015.

Congress (ANC) during his college years in return for an uncle paying his way through school. The very integrity of the students on whom he was reporting convinced him he was on the wrong side of history; he confessed and was instructed to act as a double agent until the long war against apartheid was won. This experience marked the rest of Mark's life. His novels are magnificent.[2] His friendship was precious to us.

Mark, Barbara, and I hiked a lonely trail to this site, where images that may have been 5,000 years old looked as if they'd been painted yesterday. Climate is credited with this astonishing preservation, but I have to believe the power of the figures themselves play a role in keeping them alive.

2. *The Smell of Apples* (1993) and *Embrace* (2001) are among the best known.

91

Maasai Collar, Kenya

IN KENYA AND TANZANIA, we visited Maasai communities. I cannot say I have ever been in the presence
of people to whom I felt more attracted or less connected
to at one and the same time. They welcomed us warmly,
as would be true of most gracious native peoples eager to
sell their wares to outsiders in return for giving up a bit of
privacy and a normal day's routine. They live in circles
of cow-dung homes, and cattle is their livelihood. They
wage a constant struggle to keep their valuable herds from
being eaten by lions. The Maasai people are known for
jumping high from a standing position, something they
do frequently as they sing and dance. They wear earrings

that stretch large holes in their earlobes and pull their ears into an elongated shape. The men wear loin cloths and bright wrap-around blankets and carry spears. Women as well as men adorn their necks with beautifully beaded collars. These collars are most often purchased by tourists as objects used by a people whose lives we cannot begin to understand.

92

Broken Arch, Ramesseum, Egypt

IS THE OBJECT I TREASURE the memory of these two halves of a broken arch or the open sky between them?

93

Library of Celsus, Ephesus, Turkey

ONLY THE FACADE OF the famous library still stands. My eyes linger on the numerous details of its fine carving. Then I began to listen to the stories: how the imposing structure was built in the second century BC, how a brothel was just across the way and some undecipherable relationship seems to have existed between visiting women for sex and reading the library's 12,000 scrolls, the complex ways in which the library, in its time, was the center of everyday life.

94

Uxmal, Mexico

THE MAYA OF WHAT are now southern Mexico, Guatemala, Honduras, Belize, and El Salvador are the ancient people who most attract me. Their culture dazzles. Of the dozens of Mayan ruins that we've visited, Uxmal is one of those where I've felt most at home. Uxmal and Palenque. Both sites seem to guard mysteries not yet explained in archaeological texts. And they are not deluged by visitors like the ruins of Chichén Itzá or Tikal, nor small and half devoured by jungle like Kabah or Labná. Uxmal's vast expanse is carefully tended yet retains an aura of what it must have been like when its original inhabitants crowded its plazas and worshipped in its temples. Every moment at Uxmal was precious to me.

THROUGH BROKEN SHARDS OF EARTH

— To Mexico, always dying, always rebirthing itself.

Ghosts cross my path, their voices resonate
in the conch I hold to my ear.
No tower of Babel
keeps me from their murmur,
millennial fever compressed
in this breath we share.
The woman is tunic-thin, curiosity
sparking fires inside her skull.
This *copal* air carries her off
on the wings of a dark bird.
A child's energy hits walls six-feet thick
then rebounds to trap him in his century.
On any street the amaranth of ancient stone
utters words like arrows
that hit as each sun descends
only to fly back
the following dawn,
and fade the next.
I watch their bodies move, try
to decipher their stories
echoing through broken shards of earth:
what shifting corner stones,
flawless song and the shudder
of tectonic movement leave behind.
Centuries beyond her life, Sor Juana stares at me
or Frida laughs and swings her missing leg.
Their eyes question my time as I do theirs.

Men sing beneath a weight of pumice,
their chant strumming my pulse
when I fail to caress its silence.
Broken membranes separate these layers
of burning time
and faces glow in half-light.
Echoing pigments claim my memory
like 15th century flowers hold their colors
in the burial cysts, *ofrendas* all.
You who gouged them with obsidian knives,
marriage slavery
or blood that ran thick as tears,
you who sent those tanks
rolling onto a campus of active hope
or burn today's children and hide their bodies:
You are the same as they are the same
and we are the same,
finding our torturous ways
up through layers of earth and consciousness
ready to hold on and rewind
our rebel histories.[1]

---

1. *She Becomes Time* (San Antonio: Wings Press, 2016). 100–101.

95

Great Gallery, Utah

THE 210-FOOT PANEL OF painted figures in a shallow rock alcove in central Utah may be as many as 10,000 years old. Estimates have varied wildly. The approach isn't easy. You must drive to the tiny crossroads community of Hanksville, then travel another thirty miles or so, part of the way on a dirt road, to a trailhead that begins at the edge of a cliff. An 800-foot drop to the canyon floor is listed as strenuous, but I found the rest of the six-mile hike more arduous because it follows the soft sand of a dry riverbed in mostly exposed country. Once, our progress was cut short when a sudden torrential rain caught us unprepared. On another occasion, we made it to the rock art site without meeting anyone along the way, only to find a Boy Scout troop there when we arrived.

Many of the painted figures are larger than life. Small heads sit atop long shapeless bodies with no limbs but intricate interior designs. Along with these monumental ghost-like bodies, there is a smaller duo of two people fighting and a mouth- or vagina-like symbol spewing a long line of tiny marks that seem to represent all of humanity.

96

Kiet Seel, Arizona

IT HAD LONG BEEN a dream of mine to hike into
Kiet Seel, an Ancestral Puebloan ruin at Navajo National
Monument in northern Arizona. The monument, jointly
managed by the United States National Park Service and
the Navajo Nation, contains three ruin sites. Inscription
House has been closed to the public for years; it is considered too delicate to withstand the incursion of visitors.
Betatakin is probably the best-known ruin in the park;
guided tours take place twice a day during the summer
season and we have taken one several times. I remember
on one such tour, each time someone asked a question
our Navajo guide would preface his answer: "Well, anthropologists claim such and such, the Hopi say such and
such, but we Navajo know such and such."

And then there is Kiet Seel. Years ago, you could make the trip on horseback. That's no longer allowed because the horses, too, damaged the environs. Now the only access is by foot, between late May and early September, nine miles each way over challenging terrain. You must arrive at the park the day before and attend an afternoon orientation meeting, at which you are given instructions regarding the hike and issued a permit that you have to display at all times. I pinned ours to my backpack, but no one ever saw it as far as I knew.

Barbara, our dear friend Mark, Peg Jennings, her partner at the time Shawna Swiss, and I planned our trip carefully. After attending the orientation meeting, we got rooms at the nearest motel and slept early. At dawn the following day, we all drove to the trailhead. Mark, Peggy, and I took leave of the others and started into the canyon. Our two partners would make a shorter day hike and meet us when we emerged the following afternoon.

Mark, with his athletic build, strength, and experience, carried seventy pounds to my twenty. I had prepared carb- and protein-heavy food for our dinner that night and breakfast and lunch the following day. We each carried two gallons of water, most of which Mark stored along the way in places he knew he would remember on our way out. There was no trail per se, only small wooden stakes with the number of miles and half-miles already traveled carved into them. We had to cross and re-cross a dry riverbed where we'd been warned we would have to navigate patches of quicksand. At one point we somehow got lost. Mark left the two of us behind while he went ahead to scout the way. As a child in his native South Africa, he had grown up on a wildlife refuge where he had learned scouting skills.

We only passed one other hiker that day. It was mid-afternoon when we arrived at the small campground consisting of a half-dozen sites marked with stones, and a solar-heated toilet. We dropped our packs and walked back across the river—narrow but filled with water here—to a Hogan where we knew a guide would be alert to our presence. We coughed loudly, as a way of getting his attention. Soon, a young Navajo man emerged, ready to lead us up a seventy-foot vertical ladder into the ruin itself.

The next two hours were magical. Part of Kiet Seel's attraction is that some of the pottery and implements found there have been left on site. Decorated pots, bits of hand-made rope, corncobs chewed clean eight hundred years before, even piles of petrified human excrement: evidence of the lives lived in this place. From the interior of the ruin you look down on the delta where people grew corn, beans, and squash. Then out at the canyon beyond, through which we'd just hiked. In the ruin itself, pictographs adorned some of the back walls. High on the ledge, at the alcove's entrance, the long trunk of a pine tree had been placed. This didn't seem to be as much about private property as about a community whose people had just departed. Who knew when they might be back?

Our guide told us that he was from near Monument Valley, in southern Utah. His grandfather didn't really like it that he had this job taking outsiders into a place still inhabited by the spirits of the ancestors. He, on the other hand, loved it. Each year, when he left home to work here during the summer season, his grandfather would perform a special ceremony asking the spirits to forgive him his intrusions.

After our allotted time inside the ruin, we said good-bye to our guide and returned to the campground where we'd left our backpacks and tent. I remember how cold it got that night. The only available warmth was inside the spotless toilet structure; its solar panels stored the day's heat. The next morning, we set out early on our return hike. Images and feelings remained with me as I struggled to cover the distance in reverse. Climbing up out of the canyon was especially difficult for me. I'd recently been diagnosed with emphysema and knew if I didn't make that hike when I did, it was less and less likely I would ever be able to make it. Spotting Barbara's welcoming figure just past the trailhead was a joyous moment.

> [...] Eight thousand years ago
> people some call Desert Culture
> left evidence
> of problem and solution.
> As Rome fought the Macedonian wars
> on the other side of the world
> the ancient ones set up residence in these canyons.
> From where did they come?
> Up through the Sipapu
> they tell us—passage
> from third to this fourth
> and final place.
> From the north, our experts contend:
> speculation at best.

Decision, I say.
They chose a place of sustenance
and beauty,
telling us in the shape and placement
of a window
beauty was also sustenance for them.[1]

---

1. From "Kiet Seel," in *Stones Witness*, (Tucson: University of Arizona Press, 2007), 13–14.

97

Storyteller Doll, Ada Suina, Cochiti Pueblo, New Mexico

STORYTELLER DOLLS ARE fashioned by artists, usually women, at several Rio Grande Valley pueblos. The first storyteller is believed to have been made by Helen Cordero of Cochiti. Cordero started out working in leather but switched to clay and said she produced her first doll in 1964. The origin of the figure reflects the importance of storytelling in the Native tradition but soon caught the interest of collectors and began to be seen at pueblo fairs and in upscale Santa Fe shops. Like all Native art, the statues have straddled the fine line between authentic tradition and tourist demand.

Storytellers can be several feet high and have a dozen or more children clinging to them in various places and positions. I fell in love with this one, made by Aida Suina, also of Cochiti. It sits on a shelf to the right of my writing desk. Sometimes it tells me stories, but it's possible that I talk more often to it.

98

Scissors and Ribbon,
Beat & Beyond, New York City

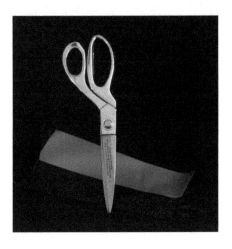

BEAT & BEYOND WAS a delirious gathering of aging beat poets and younger people inspired by the tradition. It was organized by Bob Holman of Bowery Poetry & Science and Jane Friedman of Howl! Arts, and took place in New York City in June 2016. I was invited and was one of the few still alive and capable of traveling among those men and women who called ourselves beat poets or were loosely connected to that movement in the 1950s and '60s.

Many beats were long gone. Allen Ginsberg had been dead almost a decade, Jack Kerouac since 1969. Lawrence Ferlinghetti, living and still active on the west coast, was too old to make the trip. Diane di Prima, also in San Francisco, was too ill. Michael McClure[1] showed up, as did Hettie Jones who still lives in New York, and a few others. Steven Taylor, a boy when the original beats were changing America's culture, recreated the musical group "The Fugs" and brought back some of the iconic music of the era. Other attendees had various connections to the movement.

For a week we participated in readings, panels, and lectures. We reveled in films about some of the movement's stellar figures and attended concerts that took us back in time. The event's organizers wisely lodged us all at the Standard Hotel; all we had to do was stroll with our various walking aids a few blocks down The Bowery to take in the variety of activities. At Howl! Arts, we were able to thumb through a number of books, journals, and broadsides with work by the original beats. On a white board, we lovingly wrote the names of recently departed poets and artists. One evening we recreated Ginsberg's 1955 reading of "Howl" at the Six Gallery in San Francisco. Michael McClure was the only person alive who'd taken part in the poem's first reading; in New York, he played the part of Philip Lamantia. Hettie Jones, at less than five feet, played Ginsberg. She did so with gusto.

One night we were each given a large pair of scissors with which to cut a ribbon simulating the old red and black typewriter ribbons each of us remembered from those years. My scissors and length of ribbon are objects I treasure.

As I was writing these lines, I received an unexpected phone call from Jane Friedman. She explained that Howl!

---

1. Michael McClure, 1932–2020.

Arts has a jukebox in the alley behind the gallery, where passersby push buttons and get to listen to poems read by the poets who wrote them. Could they use one of mine, she asked; they'd recorded it during my reading at Beat & Beyond. The name of the poem is "I Cannot Speak for the Gun." I was delighted. The best way to extend the life of a poem is by hearing it in the poet's voice. The Beats keep on changing America, not only its literary culture but its way of looking at the world.

I CANNOT SPEAK FOR THE GUN

I cannot speak for the gun
doing its ugly job
in George Zimmerman's overeager hands.
I cannot speak for those eighteen ounces
easily concealed in a killer's pocket.
Easy to guess what George's intention was,
too easy to imagine the terror
in Trayvon's eyes,
the grief his mother holds
years beyond her loss.
The Law never found Zimmerman guilty
or condemned his crime.
And Martin could not know
his death would bring a nation
into the streets
or that hundreds of other black youth
would have to die, gunned down
by white policemen
or self-styled protectors

of an order that runs by exception
in this country where Law protects
the men who write it, works
for white, fails for black, rich
or poor, genders
that matter or don't.
Now George Zimmerman auctions
the gun that murdered
Trayvon Martin. He's asking
$5,000, promises some of the money
will go to fight Black Lives Matter
because, simply put, they don't matter
to him. Will this gun's new home
turn its barrel around
or lure another trigger finger
in wait?
I cannot speak for the gun or the men
who love caressing its fever.
My job is finding the words
that describe the weapon's threat
precisely.[1]

---

1. *The Morning After: Poetry and Prose in a Post-Truth World* (San Antonio: Wings Press, 2017), 37.

99

When Justice Felt at Home / Cuando la justicia se sentía en casa, Handmade Vigía Book, Cuba

VIGÍA OCCUPIES A two-story colonial house on a small triangular plaza in the Cuban city of Matanzas. In 1985, Matanzas poet Alfredo Zaldívar gained access to what had been the city's Casa del Escritor. Stage-set designer Rolando Estévez joined Zaldívar, and a group of writers and artists began talking about creating a collective through which they could promote their work. Their first publications were invitations and playbills for local theatrical and musical productions. It wasn't long before they started making books.

Life in Cuba wasn't easy in the mid to late '80s and into the '90s. The 1989 implosion of the Soviet bloc had produced debilitating shortages. Fidel Castro dubbed the era a Special Period in a Time of Peace. The difficulties of everyday life sent thousands of Cubans emigrating; 125,000 alone had departed in the Mariel boatlift of 1980. It was in this painful context that Vigía was born. Its founders have always insisted that choosing to make books out of materials you can find in the street didn't respond as much to the scarcity of the era as it did to their desire to create beauty out of found objects.

Vigía has never owned a printing press. All work on each title's two hundred copies is done on an aging mimeograph machine and by hand. The collective has published books by authors whose work has been repressed from time to time within the Cuban Revolution's up and down history of censorship. Many important gay writers or those who have written about issues not always favored by the revolutionary leadership have seen their books produced in beautiful editions by Vigía. The truth is, every Cuban writer and many from around the world hope to have a Vigía edition.

I am fortunate to have two books published by Vigía. The first was a bilingual edition of *La Llorona*, translated into Spanish by María Vázquez Valdez, edited by Laura Ruiz Montes, and designed by Elizabeth Valero. The second is the one pictured here: *When Justice Felt at Home / Cuando la justicia se sentía en casa*. It is a suite of six poems about contemporary Cuba. This is also a bilingual edition. The Spanish translation is by Katherine M. Hedeen and Víctor Rodríguez Núñez, and the edition and design are once again by Ruiz Montes and Valero.

The book is bound in ordinary jute, the kind used in wholesale grain bags. At the bottom, beneath my name, is a weave of cane used in traditional Cuban furniture. The replica of the square tile just above this appears in six different designs throughout the two hundred copies, each tile adorning thirty-three or thirty-four of them.

Vigía sells its books at modest prices to Cubans and at higher prices in convertible currency to people around the world. Many Vigía books are in museums and private collections. Zaldívar and Estévez have both moved on to other projects, and new people are keeping the Vigía experience going.

100

Haydée Santamaría Medal, Cuba

IT'S LATE MAY IN BOSTON. I am receiving the Haydée Santamaría medal, the highest honor Cuba's Casa de las Américas bestows upon "writers and artists of prestigious trajectories who have had a close intellectual relationship with Cuba and with Casa." It is customary for Casa to give the medal to recipients at the Cuban embassy in their respective countries. In the case of the United States, Trump has made that impossible, so the ceremony is taking place in the context of the Latin American Studies Association (LASA), held this year in Boston. Although the US government has refused visas to the majority of Cuba's LASA delegation, several are able to be here. A panel on *El Corno Emplumado* fifty years from its demise has kindly allowed us to take its last fifteen minutes to hold this ceremony.

Jaime García Triana, Director of Casa's Original Cultures of America Department, reads the official proclamation of Cuba's Counsel of State. He speaks movingly about the heroine, and I realize that she died before he was born; he never knew the woman but, like almost every Cuban, knows what she represents. Then he speaks about me. I think of the sixty-six men and women from all over the Americas, some of them friends, who received it before: great Cuban prima ballerina Alicia Alonso, Uruguayan poet and novelist Mario Benedetti, Brazilian Dominican brother and liberation theologian Frei Betto, deposed Dominican Republic president Juan Bosch, Nicaraguan priest and poet Ernesto Cardenal, Uruguayan writer and philosopher Eduardo Galeano, Colombian novelist Gabriel García Márquez, Argentine poet Juan Gelman, Ecuadoran painter and sculptor Oswaldo Guayasamín, Cuban Minister of Culture Armando Hart, Chilean painter Roberto Matta, Argentine book publisher Arnaldo Orfila, Haitian economist and author Gerard Pierre-Charles, Cuban singer/songwriter Silvio Rodríguez, Argentine singer/songwriter Mercedes Sosa, Peruvian anthropologist Stefano Varese, Uruguayan singer/songwriter Daniel Viglietti, and poet Idea Vilariño.

Many are gone now, some are still with us, yet all seem to accompany me at this moment. Benedetti and Viglietti were family friends. I knew Cardenal in Mexico City in the heady 1960s before he became a priest, and later worked with him at the Sandinista Ministry of Culture in the early 1980s. Arnaldo Orfila was a close friend and one of my first

editors when he headed Siglo XXI, a publishing house
I and hundreds of others helped him establish when, as
longtime director of El Fondo de Cultura Económica, he
had been removed from his position for publishing two
books that angered the Mexican government in the mid-
1960s. Silvio Rodríguez sometimes dropped by our apartment in Havana, even as he and a few others were creating
Cuba's powerful New Song Movement. Stefano Varese
and I worked together in Peru in 1974 when Juan Velasco
Alvarado was in power; we reconnected in Cuba in 2011,
were both invited to judge Casa's yearly literary contest,
and he accompanies me here now. A family of likeminded
writers, artists, and performers who believed we could help
bring justice to a world that would betray our dreams.

Some lived to see that betrayal. Others didn't.

Then my memory goes to the woman for whom this
medal is named. Haydée took her own life in 1980. I think
she may have seen the coming of the end. Or at least the
end this time around, for I have not lost hope—and I don't
believe she did either—in humanity's eventual ability to
live in creativity and peace.

Following their 1959 victory, Fidel Castro charged
Haydée with establishing Casa de las Américas, an arts
institution capable of combatting the US cultural blockade that promised to be as daunting and damaging as its
military, economic, and diplomatic counterparts. There
were those who wondered at the choice. Why tap a poorly-
educated woman who knew nothing of art and literature
for a post that could have been filled by one of the many
prestigious artists who supported the new government?
Haydée wasted no time in proving she was the ideal per-

son for the job. She quickly taught herself about the arts. And she possessed a deep sensibility that allowed her to identify with the world's great writers and artists, whose idiosyncrasies weren't that different from her own.

So many creative people were introduced to the Cuban Revolution through Haydée. I was one of them. My first visit to the island was in response to Casa's invitation to a gathering of poets celebrating the hundredth anniversary of the great Nicaraguan modernist Rubén Darío. Haydée embraced us all. I can't forget my first impression of that modest-looking woman, slightly bent from chronic asthma. Her vivid blue eyes pierced yours and never strayed as you conversed. She went straight to the grain, giving you to understand she was profoundly interested in everything you could tell her about yourself. Her passion was contagious. Beneath a wildly creative sense of humor lived the desperation that came from having lost those she'd loved most. Today we call it PTSD; back then we didn't have a word for it. What was most obvious about Haydée was her implacable sense of justice. She sought it in everything she did and brought it out in everyone she met.

When my family and I moved to Cuba in 1969, Haydée became a friend and mentor. She was one of three or four mentors I've been fortunate enough to have in my life, a great honor and privilege. I was invited to judge the poetry category at Casa's 1970 literary contest and observed her interactions with the other judges, listened as she urged us to put aside political considerations and evaluate each book solely on its literary merits. In the years I lived in Cuba, I watched as she shaped Casa into one of the preeminent cultural institutions in the Americas, as truly democratic in its internal workings as it is respected in the wider world. All these years later, Haydée's spirit still inhabits every corner of the building.

Many years later, long after leaving Cuba, living in Nicaragua, and returning to my native United States, I realized that I had to write about Haydée. Not a biography as much as an appreciation; but enough of a biography to introduce her to those outside Cuba who had never heard her name. *Haydée Santamaría: Cuban Revolutionary. She Led by Transgression* was published by Duke University Press in 2015. I could not have imagined then, nor do I quite believe now, that I would one day be wearing the medal that bears her name.

Gómez Triana has finished and Suilán Rodríguez Trasancos steps forward, bearing a small wooden box. Suilán is Casa's Vice President for Economics, another member of Cuba's LASA delegation who managed to make the trip. As she pins the medal to my sweater, I think of the heroine, thank her for having lived. But I whisper to the old friend: *"Tu pelo se ve hermoso,"* I assure her, remembering how concerned she always was about her hair.

Lightning Source UK Ltd.
Milton Keynes UK
UKHW020934120920
369709UK00005B/33

9 781613 321140